PROUD [illegible]

Barbara Anderson is t[illegible] *Portrait of the Artist's* [illegible] Award), *All the Nice* G[illegible] *Guest* and *Proud Garments*, and a collect[illegible] of stories, *I think we should go into the jungle.*

BY BARBARA ANDERSON

I think we should go into the jungle
Girls High
Portrait of the Artist's Wife
All the Nice Girls
The House Guest
Proud Garments

Barbara Anderson

PROUD GARMENTS

Published by Vintage 1998

2 4 6 8 10 9 7 5 3 1

First published in Great Britain by
Jonathan Cape, 1997

Vintage
Random House, 20 Vauxhall Bridge Road,
London SW1V 2SA

Random House Australia (Pty) Limited
20 Alfred Street, Milsons Point, Sydney
New South Wales 2061, Australia

Random House New Zealand Limited
18 Poland Road, Glenfield,
Auckland 10, New Zealand

Random House South Africa (Pty) Limited
Endulini, 5A Jubilee Road, Parktown 2193,
South Africa

Random House UK Limited Reg. No. 954009

A CIP catalogue record for this book
is available from the British Library

ISBN 0 09 976281 1

Papers used by Random House UK Ltd are natural, recyclable products made from wood grown in sustainable forests. The manufacturing processes conform to the environmental regulations of the country of origin

Printed and bound in Great Britain by
Mackays of Chatham plc, Chatham, Kent

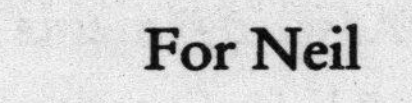

For Neil

Acknowledgements

This novel was written with the assistance of a grant from Creative New Zealand.

My grateful thanks also to Marilyn Sainty, Lise Strathdee and Dorothea Turner for all their help.

one

'There's a dead bird outside my bedroom window,' said Bianca. 'It's been there for some time.'

Rosa looked at her sister in silence. You wouldn't read about it. You simply would not read about it. 'Oh. Did you hear that, Henry?'

Henry Felton, morose and silent, was busy with doggerel. Hark hark, is that a sparrow carking / Or merely our Bianca farting. 'Yes,' he said, 'I did. And God already has.'

Bianca stirred in her tub chair. What did she have to do to achieve action in this house—kick? roar? scream? She spoke with emphasis.

'For quite some time,' she said. 'A sparrow.'

Henry continued his fight with the paper. One of those bits, those infuriating, unwanted, uncalled for *bits* fell at his feet. Vanity units were on special.

'Dead birds butter no parsnips,' he muttered.

'What's that supposed to mean?'

'I've no idea.' Henry rubbed his nose, a large, aquiline nose pinched about the bridge. A Roman nose, good for show, not for blow. 'There are many aphorisms I don't understand. *If the shoe fits wear it.* What's that supposed to mean?'

Bianca bent forward, gave a low husky laugh, a sound

forced from her by her brother-in-law's inability to tackle problems as they arose. To seize the day, the nettle, the hour. Unlike her late husband, Henry has no grip at all. Justin Lefarge had been trained to make decisions in a disciplined environment; to diagnose, to prescribe, to cure. His career as a psychologist in the Royal Army Medical Corps had been distinguished; change and decay had come as a surprise to him. His demise had been prolonged and Bianca had nursed him to the end. Letters from Hampshire to Meadowbank had been full of praise. *Dear Mrs Felton, I thought I should let you know how much we all admire your sister's courage and fortitude at this sad time . . .*

'It's quite simple, Henry, and anyway it's the cap, not the shoe. It merely means . . .' Bianca stopped; silent, appalled, her brain turned to mush. What did it mean? Which cap? Why wear it? She clenched the hands hidden among folds of navy and white, sat straighter and breathed again, blessed the saving grace of rational thought as it flowed once more. 'If I say you're being stupid and you are, you must accept my saying so. You must wear the cap that fits you, that's all. It's a metaphor. Shakespeare. The Maoris. *A mighty totara has fallen.* You should know that. You're the ones who live here.'

As indeed they did and did and do. Henry and me, and Bianca makes three. Rosalind avoided her husband's eye, rubbed her itchy thumb.

By the pricking of my thumbs something something this way comes.

But which crone is it? Witch one, two or three? Mother would have known. She was grateful for the works of William Shakespeare who, she told her two small daughters, had saved her sanity when Father died.

She had founded the Meadowbank branch of the Shakespeare Society and owned the concordance which is now Rosa's. She had organised play readings in her house around the corner, had quoted soliloquies and sonnets and heroic blood stirrers as they drove to Pukekohe to pick their own tomatoes and Bianca said she was sick of PYO and why did they have to. '*Stiffen the sinews, summon up the blood,*' cried Mother, as they swung in to park by the packing shed. 'Besides, they're cheaper.'

Mother had chosen their names from her hero's work with care. The tragedies had not been consulted. Desdemona, Cordelia, Ophelia, although euphonious words and fine women all, were impossible, irreparably damaged names.

Rosalind, however, did not suit. Its recipient's lack of height for one thing. The baby grew into a tiny scrap of a child with blue-black eyes and wispy dark hair. She became Rosa, or worse, Ros, neither of which suited her but what could you do.

Bianca remained Bianca. Now Bianca Lefarge, sitting in the small chair with the sun behind her, pretty as a picture beneath the pompom dahlias in a trough on the mantelpiece. The dahlias are the same crimson-cherry as the beaks of black swans, their ovoid petals resemble the feathers ruffled like the petticoats of cancan dancers but black as soot. They are mysterious, seductive animals, black swans, more so than the white.

Rosalind is also fond of the pottery trough. Bianca did not want anything from the house when Mother died, except, of course, the silver and something more personal, some more intimate remembrance. Her pearls would do. Bianca had her own things, she wrote, and besides, her taste had changed.

Rosalind looked at her sister. Bianca is well preserved, if you can stand the phrase, but not mummified. Fifty-five if a day and not a wrinkle in sight.

Laughter is bad for the face and not having children helps as well. They should put it on packets, like health warnings. Cereal perhaps, something seen every day so the effect is cumulative. *Families may endanger your face.* Rosa thought of her son Rufus and stopped quickly. Years ago a Christian on a bicycle had pressed Alexander Pope's words in tract form into her hands before pedalling on down the tree-lined street. *To err is human, to forgive, divine . . .*

Not that Rufus has erred exactly. In fact not at all. Rosa's thoughts skidded and returned to Mother.

Mother serene and cheerful in her navy straw and her dark silk speckled like the guinea fowl in the children's zoo. So many worries, so little money and always pleasant. Mother bending stiffly from the waist to enquire after her friends in Smith and Caugheys. Mother in the tearooms afterwards, her shopping done, her face wrinkled as a pleated skirt but still handsome. Mother in gloves and hat walking home from the Meadowbank bus stop one day to be bowled over by a taxi at the corner.

It was the greengrocer who had broken the news to Rosalind. Mr Desai had dropped the apple he was polishing and run to her, had taken the spade from her hands and led her inside. 'Sit down Mrs, oh sit down. Your lovely lady is dead.' She wept in his arms till Henry appeared, wept as though the Waitemata had ceased to flow and Meadowbank was no more and life had ended. Mother had gone.

She telephoned Bianca that evening. It was morning there.

'Did she ask for me?'

'No, no, dear, she was killed instantly.'

'*Instantly.*'

As though that made it worse.

Bianca resembles Mother except for her unlined face; even her seated shape is similar—the spreading hips, the shapely legs. Mother was soft to the touch, spongy almost above the waist. 'It has to go somewhere, Rosa,' she laughed, as the child poked the pallid tube above her girdle.

Below the waist she was firmer, constrained, subdued by latex even after Lionel died. He had been a good man, she told them, and a great tease and had liked her firm. Besides, she hated to flop about. Rosalind was seven when he died but her memories of her father are few: bony knees, a pipe, the pleasures of bonfires. Not much, in all conscience, and Bianca has no memories at all.

Like many larger women, Mother had elegant feet and ankles. They lightened her, she seemed to sail above them as does Bianca, who has the same walk, a slow, graceful surge forward. She does not scamper from task to task like her older sister. Bianca appears to stream along, to billow like the scarves she favours. (Bianca is a scarf person.) The carp kites which fly from Japanese houses in celebration of a son's birthday reminded Rosalind of them both.

The kites are a fine sight; anchored yet free, they lift the heart. Daughters do not have them. Rosalind, with Henry on a buying trip, had asked the interpreter what girls do have. There was something she cannot remember, dolls perhaps, but nothing airborne, nothing as triumphantly buoyant.

The three of them are quiet now, mellow as the afternoon sun warming Bianca's shoulders. Henry's feet continue to grind the carpet as he reads the book reviews.

Bianca sits thinking about her things. Her eyes move, her mind ticks. How can she fit them all into a room this size, even when Ros has got rid of all this stuff. Bianca's gaze checks spaces, areas, height (the longcase clock), rips down curtains and throws out sofas. Her shoulders move in a minuscule shudder at the worn florals, the flowers and the leaves and the songbirds singing on the ancient slip covers, the tired cushions and neo-colonial tat. Tat was a word much used by Barry at Arnold's Antiques in Fareham, Hants. Bianca tries it, her lips moving in silence. Tat.

And the dog trade. She saw Barry, his trim behind giving a little sideways shimmy as he edged past a badly cracked garden urn. 'Dog trade, Mrs L. Strictly dog trade.'

'Dog trade?'

'People who're putting on the dog. All hair oil and no socks.'

Oh, the joys of exclusion when you weren't, and where was Arnold's Antiques now and Barry who was such fun and knew the importance of contemporary armorials and that Mrs L had a wonderful eye and was not and never had been dog trade. Twelve thousand miles away and sadly missed, that was where. Sadly, sadly missed.

But Bianca's container is due to arrive in a few months. Her things are on their way.

'*Speed bonnie boat like a bird on the wing*,' she sings softly her head tilting from side to side. Bianca often sings softly.

'Don't *cross* on the solid white *line*,' she sang from the front passenger's seat when they picked her up from the airport. 'Full stop ahead.'

'Yellow,' snarled Henry. 'Double yellow. You're home now.' Bianca turned her face to the window, to bleached paddocks and wire fences and silly sheep huddling.

She was more robust when Ros drove, blocking her vision as she peered left, shouting, 'Now! I said now. Why didn't you go?'

'Because I can't see.'

'Of course you can't see. I can. You can scarcely see over the steering wheel. You need a cushion. That elf one would do, that extraordinary elf one on the sofa.'

Rosalind drew in to the side and stopped the car. Her normally brown face was pale, she was breathing fast. 'Bianca, it's time we had a team talk. That's what they call them. They go into a huddle on TV and have team talks.' Her hands sketched stadiums, snarling coaches and intrusive cameras.

'I have been driving a car for more than forty years and intend to continue doing so. And furthermore, Bianca,' said Rosalind, staring straight at her, her eyes sparking, positively sparking, 'we didn't ask you to come and live with us.'

Bianca burst into tears. 'What a terrible thing to say to your sister.'

'Yes, isn't it,' said Rosa and drove on to the asparagus farm where it was always fresh and half the price.

Rosa had come scuttling back to bed the night Bianca arrived. 'She goes to bed in gloves,' she told Henry, who was lying with his eyes closed. 'Gloves on top of hand cream. Little cotton ones.'

There was something about gloves and fat women and nobody loving but Henry was too tired. Too tired and too depressed. Rosa rolled towards him, her face suddenly serious. 'Henry. Don't die in the night.'

Henry's eyes had opened. 'All right,' he said, and closed them again.

Bianca was still singing to herself.

Speed bonnie boat, like a bird on the wing
'Onward,' the sailors cry!
Carry the lad that's born to be King
Over the sea to Skye.

'A Jacobite, a genuine, fully paid up Jacobite in Meadowbank,' sniffed Henry.

Bianca looked at him warily. Her eyes, less blue than formerly but still sharp, met his. No, thought Henry, not sharp. Her gaze is knowing. He had met only one other woman in his life who had looked at him like that and she was dead. Dead and buried and laid to rest in Milan. Bianca should not look at him like that. She had no right. He stared out the window. Anywhere to avoid Bianca.

She made no comment on his asinine remark. She was no fool. He knew that.

Shadows and silence filled the room, deepened the crimson dahlias, bent the heads of host and hostess. Henry shifted slightly, tossed a cushion to the floor and worked himself deeper into cretonne.

Bianca broke the silence. Her voice was clear. She had a good ear and thirty years in Titchfield had left their mark.

'I'm sure you won't mind my mentioning it, Henry . . .' she said, leaning forward to stare into his eyes. Brown eyes are meant to be warm but nothing about Henry was predictable. 'But I've wondered so often. Well, you can imagine. And Justin as well. Was anything more ever discovered about Andrew's death?'

Henry's mouth dropped in disbelief. 'What do you mean, discovered? You know exactly what happened. He was drowned while fishing. Slipped and fell over the Huka Falls thirty-three years ago.'

'Rufus was two,' offered Rosalind.

Neither of them glanced at her.

'Yes, yes, of course,' said Bianca, flustered but firm. 'But nothing . . . Was nothing more ever heard about . . .' She faltered, tried again. 'About the reason for his taking his life.'

'Taking his life! You say that? You of all people.'

'It seems so odd.'

'In what way?'

'To be fishing there.'

There was a red blotch between his eyebrows. 'Are you mad? How could anyone fish at the Huka Falls? He slipped further upstream and was swept over. Death by misadventure, as you very well know.'

Bianca drew back. I have gone too far. Far too far because I dislike him. That awful mother, that ridiculous father, all of them. Why shouldn't I bring it up. The way I was treated, the cover-up. Everything. Justin had been appalled.

But that face, that beaked, stained face thrust at hers, those cold eyes. She could see the hairs in his nostrils, the hairs beside the hairs, the damp redness.

'I'm sorry, Henry. I didn't mean to imply . . .'

'What in heaven's name is there to imply?'

'Nothing, nothing. I'm sorry. I've said I'm sorry.'

Henry flopped back in his chair. 'And so am I.' He breathed deeply, felt his heart slow, find its own rhythm and quieten.

'My apologies, Bianca. But for God's sake let Andy rot in peace.' The newspaper sighed beneath his hands and lay quiet. 'Though I suppose he has by now.'

Sun filtered, motes of dust hung in slanting rays of unease and silence. 'Perhaps I should have said dead birds don't squeak,' he muttered.

The man was shifty and devious beyond belief. How Ros had ever been able to contemplate the thought of matrimony, let alone live forty years with a man like Henry Felton was beyond comprehension. He bore no resemblance to his younger brother. None. The textiles he imported were beautiful, Bianca would give him that, but what use were they with his wife sitting staring at her in crumpled cotton you could shoot peas through. Ros had no dress sense. Not an ounce.

Bianca had enjoyed her marriage and her life in England. She had drifted onto the local pond like a decoy, had displayed the right markings and been accepted by the indigenous flock. She had kept her own counsel on many things and it had been wonderfully, gloriously worth it, and now look at her. All money gone, all passion spent, expiring with boredom in this dump and men swearing at her.

'Incidentally,' she said, 'what about the dead bird?'

'Oh, for heaven's sake, Bianca,' said Rosa. 'Sparrows don't smell or blow up or anything. They just sort of wither. I'll give you a spade.'

Henry dragged himself to his feet and headed for the kitchen. 'What would you like to drink, Bianca?'

Bianca made a small regrouping movement. 'The one I had last night when the tonic ran out was so delicious, I think I'll have another. What was it, Henry?'

Henry's eyes closed briefly. 'Water,' he said, 'and gin.' He moved towards the kitchen, his fingers touching chairs, tables, a book, before reaching the top cupboard for the gin bottle. Rosa had once suggested changes to him. Why didn't Henry move the drink bottles into the cupboard beneath the bookcase? There would be room for the glasses and all he would need to bring in would be a jug of water. He had declined. For God's sake, he said, don't make it any easier.

Rosa watched his back as he headed for the kitchen. His self-deprecating honesty was endearing and always had been. She knew there were things about him. Undoubtedly there were. His refusal to talk about Rufus's future, for example. 'Rufus will be all right,' was all he would say. 'Don't worry about Rufus.'

His blanket denial did not leave her any room to manoeuvre, to discuss, to work things through and share.

Similarly with Bianca. It was all very well to say, 'Bianca must go', but where, and how, and anyway how could she. She has no money and she is my sister and Bianca now is Bianca then, when I was seven and she was two and I promised Mother I would mind her and did.

Henry stood with the open bottle in his hand, an old man with a dry mouth staring at a lemon tree. The lemons hung gleaming in the reflected light, their crisp leaves slicked with raindrops as bright as mercury and as separate. Any fool can grow a lemon tree in Auckland. It's simply a question of digging a big enough hole. People are mean about digging holes. Wide and deep, wide and deep, that is all that is required.

There are not many people you love. Not men. Not men like Andy, who had loved Bianca. She was now expressing doubts about the TV news presenter's beautifully white teeth. False, obviously false, too good to be true. Bianca could always tell, always, and furthermore she had never been able to trust anyone with false teeth. It was just something she had a thing about, and who did the woman think she was anyway.

'Must it *all* be sport,' she moaned, as men rolled to their feet clutching balls in triumph, and impossible putts were sunk and cups presented and held high for kissing.

Henry handed her gin.

'Thank you. I've never had it like this before, women don't in Hampshire.' She sipped, circumspect as a communicant. 'And why do they need two of them? The news is not a cabaret act.'

If I strangle her she won't know she's dead so what is the point. There is no point. There is no point at all.

Rosalind put her feet up. She was bored with opening and shutting her mouth between protagonists like a hungry fledgling. How could Bianca say that about Andy. And to Henry. My own sister, my sister who has descended on us. She saw Bianca, robed in blue and manhandled by angels, descending from clouds like a rewound Assumption. Why here? Why here? Because there is nowhere else.

'Bed,' said Henry. 'Come on, Rosa.'

Rosa looked into her husband's eyes and read his baffled heart. He was miserable and uneasy. He wanted solidarity, contact, he wanted to talk to his wife. 'Coming,' she said.

He climbed into bed, clutching striped pyjamas to his

midriff. The elastic had gone. 'And the husband was worse, *de mortuis* notwithstanding. But when she got on to Andy . . . No, Rosa . . . No.'

Rosa was drowsy, kicking the word notwithstanding around between doze and dream. Notwithstanding. Not forever.

Not forever by green pastures
Do we ask our way to be
But the sleep and rugged pathway
May we tread rejoicingly.

There is a man in Britain who climbs mountains on two aluminium alloy feet. It is the ankle joints he misses.

'What else can we do?' she murmured.

'She cannot just descend on us.'

'Don't be so daft. She has.'

'You'll have to tell her to go. I mean it, Rosa.'

'No.'

'Then I will.'

'She has no money.'

'That's dusty Justy's legacy, not mine.'

Rosa was wide awake now, her voice firm. 'She is my sister and she is penniless and she is welcome in this house till the day I die. Then you can toss her out the door. And you shouldn't have said that about rotting in peace. Things are bad enough already. Why didn't you just say rest. It was just gratuitous . . .' She stopped. Gratuitous what? Violence? Truth? 'It was cruel,' she muttered.

Henry leaned towards her in the dark to clutch her shoulders, misjudged and fell back. 'Look how she treats you. Me. The whole world. Why, woman, why?'

Ah, but how can I tell you, my lover, my friend. My sister is my responsibility and always has been. She is burnt into my software, as Rufus would say. Besides I promised.

Binky has lace on her panties and lace on her hankim. And so she had and was cherished as all children should be and are not. 'Where has Rosa gone? Poor Rosa will be missing me,' she wept, tears rolling down her nose when I went to play with Wendy down the road. So Binky came too and Wendy loved her as well and Mother rested with the blinds drawn.

'Is that your baby, dear?' Wendy's mother had asked as Bianca clutched a small round cushion to her chest.

'No,' said Bianca. 'It's my handbag.'

She refused to be a baby when Wendy and I needed one. There were no babies in our house, just Mother and me and Bianca. It was sufficient and there was much to do. Nothing happens automatically in houses, someone must clean up now and again and Mother preferred Shakespeare and Bianca the garden.

'You mustn't mind, Rosa, if no one . . .' Mother had warned before the dance. 'I mean there's always the cloakroom. Not of course that you'll . . . You look lovely, dear,' she said firmly. 'Lovely.'

When she arrived to pick me up, Henry and I were dancing with tears in our eyes. Our tears were those of laughter, but that is not so in the original song, which is a sad one. The singer's partner is not the one he loves and thus his eyes are wet. I always worried for his partner, but perhaps she didn't notice.

The look on Mother's face gladdened my heart further as Henry and I swept past. Surprise was followed by joy and joy outshone. I should have grabbed her—spun her around with us beneath the tethered balloons tugging like memories. See, I should have said. Don't worry, I should have laughed. It will be all right. I am a grown woman.

Tight buds were unfurling in the Parnell Rose Gardens, opening to butter yellow and fierce reds and pinks as Henry and I walked beside them. I agreed they were beautiful, how could I not. They were and I did not care. I scarcely noticed them except the clashing colours. Roses are the only flowers whose colours can fight.

Make Henry Felton ask me to marry him, I insisted to a lurid pink. You were allowed to then, to hope and pray for love, to consider yourself lucky if asked. I do not know why I added the Felton. Perhaps I felt it was more formal.

'Rosa, will you marry me?'

'Yes,' I said instantly. 'Yes, please.'

Henry worked for his father. Mr Felton senior's textile importing business was well established and efficiently run. It was the rest of the world which worried the old man. His expression was often bewildered, even hurt. He felt that a more 'wholesome' (that was the word he used), a more wholesome life was slipping away.

Now I tell Henry. The world has not changed, I tell him. Old people always think things used to be better, it is one of the signs of aging. And now there is communication, there is TV, there are satellites. People cannot help but see if the switch is on. They see the bombs and the bodies and the misery. They do not need to have any imagination at all. It is not only you, Henry, my darling, my friend.

When he looks at me I see that his brown eyes are still beautiful despite the opaque band around the pupil which is called *arcus senilis*. I do not tell him this.

We lie side by side, tanned and wrinkled like two connubial old kippers.

I think of Bianca and of our son Rufus who is coming home soon and how wonderful and what will he do. Of Bianca's things which she says will be arriving soon and where will they go. Bianca says this will be no problem. I do not like this phrase. I am wary of it. Often I find that, contrary to what the speaker says, there is a problem and, more often than not, it is mine. Bianca tells me I can get rid of my stuff and then there will be room. I tell her they are not stuff. I tell her they are my things but she does not agree. I will have it out with her tomorrow. Bianca, I will say.

Henry puts out a hand. 'Are you asleep?'

'No.'

'She'll have to go.'

'No.'

Henry takes me in his arms.

If I had a daughter I would tell her. Don't worry, I would say, it is just as good. It is just as good as ever. It is simply that it happens less often, I would say.

'*My love who could deliver*,' says Henry and sleeps.

There is no need to tell Rufus.

'Are you awake?' I ask later.

Even in the silent dark I know he is frowning. 'This is ridiculous. Hissing away in bedrooms at our age.'

'I've thought of a solution,' I say.

There is a muffled snort beside me.

'We must find somewhere else for Bianca to live.'

The light snaps on. We stare at each other in disarray; old, bewildered, not our daytime selves at all. Henry's hair is a fuzz of white light. He is an anguished saint, one of those attenuated Spanish ones. 'And who pays for it?'

'We could rent a nice little flat for her. A townhouse even.'

'Rosalind, have you the slightest idea how much a nice flat costs?'

I ignore the flick of distancing which comes with the use of my full name. 'Little, I said, a little flat.'

'However little.'

'I still think it would be worth discussing. I'll contact some letting agents tomorrow. Come to your office.'

'I will not pay for that . . .' He does not say it but the word hangs in the air, clings to the curtains, a spiky black snitch of a word.

He snaps off the light and we lie still.

His hand strokes my rump. 'Come anyway. Bianca,' Henry tells the dark, 'can attend to her correspondence.'

He rolls over.

'Did she really say that? About her correspondence?'

No answer.

two

Bianca pours liquid honey onto yoghurt as she has done every breakfast since she and Justin discovered Greece. The loops and swirls are precise. Like all her actions, small or large, Bianca's movements are meticulous, she likes to get things right. Seemliness, order, patterns of procedure are important to her.

She glances up as Rosalind runs back from the kitchen. 'Every time I see you you've grown smaller, you know that. There'll be nothing left soon. Remember that one at primary? *Rosie Maule is so small, a rat could eat her, cap and all.*'

'Yes,' says Rosalind spreading Vegemite, remembering the jeers and no one choosing her for goalie because she'd be useless being so minute, when she wasn't, not at all. Biting, chewing, blinking the moment to oblivion, she takes it out on toast.

And if I told her, *when* I tell her, that Bianca Lefarge is overly large she will be crushed, she will weep, will burst immediately into the hot, wounded tears of the misunderstood, the can't-take-a-jokes, the plain speakers.

'More toast?' says Rosalind and runs again.

'Not every woman can be a pocket Venus, Bianca,' says Henry.

He was handsome once, as Bianca knows, and is still impressive. His grey hair is thick and silky, the lines on his face are fine, not the deep ravines of lonely men on benches drinking out of flagons. He stands upright, giving a spurious appearance of confidence and attack.

Bianca reaches for her handkerchief. He is a fraud and I hate him. His double talk, his so-called wit, the accuracy of his jibes upset me. And now Ros, charging in and out being ridiculous in that poky little kitchen.

Bianca has a sharp tongue. She knows this and it worries her. Sometimes things she has said or done come back to haunt her. Mrs Spencer taking umbrage when she couldn't give her a lift in to Fareham because her basket might scratch the leather. Mrs Rowland and that wretched hamster. More serious things, horrible things such as Doctor Clothier's letter suggesting she find another medical adviser. Not even giving her a chance to explain, and why shouldn't she have a second opinion. I did not mean to offend, Doctor, it is just my way. I don't mean to be rude but things pop out and people have no sense of humour. They take things personally, Doctor, they cannot take a joke. There are some things would you believe, Doctor, which have stayed with me for over thirty years. Humphrey Watson leaving me stranded on the dance floor, striding off in the middle of the Excuse Me when I told him he looked like a Romney Southdown cross and he did. These are not big things, Doctor, I realise that. Nevertheless they stay with me, they return in the night.

Rosalind watched a tangerine-beaked blackbird rush an elegant thrush on the grass below. The thrush departed squawking. Good, good on you. Do it again.

She slammed the toaster lever down, remembered Saint Lawrence on his gridiron. *Turn me, devil, eat. And see if raw or toasted, I make the better meat.*

Such a help they are, her talismans. Rosalind smiles, the toast pops, life goes on. Last night's loving resurfaces and that is part of the problem. Rosalind knows she could live with Bianca more easily without Henry, although she has no intention of doing so. She knows Bianca, tries to understand her, can almost see her trying to be nice, then, wham—the boot is in, the game is over. Bianca is on form once more.

Bianca, her curls golden as those of the unborn Rufus, had sobbed in her arms over thirty-five years ago. 'People don't like me. Why Ros? Why don't some people like me?'

Rosa had had a long hot wait at the antenatal and the humidity hadn't helped.

'Men or women?'

'Women mostly.'

'Because you're beautiful,' said Rosalind, running the cold tap on the inside of her wrists as Mother had taught them because it was so cooling. She scowled at the red face at the bottom of the mirror. All mirrors were too high.

'Oh,' said Bianca. She paused. 'But I can't help that.'

Rosa was now slapping water on her face. 'No. It's tough, being a beautiful woman. Ask Elsa Maxwell. She organised parties for millionaires and all their dolly birds loved her. She was plain, plain as a pikestaff, plain as the east end of a camel going west. She'd got no class, see, she wasn't sexy, but she gave ace parties and she made you crack up laughing and why not love the funny old doll? She was no threat. It just depends,' said Rosa, rubbing her face on a lilac towel, 'whether you want to be a millionaire's doxy or organise his parties.'

Doxy. Doxy was typical of Ros. One of those words you know exists but no one in their right mind would use. A word used only by funny girls like Rosa. As were her hats. No one had worn hats then. No one young. No one but Ros. Where did she find them, those mad little black hats with turned-up brims which made her look smaller than ever; a squat mushroom with a fringe of hair and dark eyes staring.

'Oh, Rosa, what would I do without you?' cried Bianca.

The toast flew upwards like sparks and trouble. Shakespeare.

Bianca and Henry were sitting in silence, an angry silence, which was rare in the house. Silences, as a rule, were amiable. There was not much chat, the permanent residents knew each other too well, their reactions were demonstrated by a nod, acknowledged by an eyebrow. There were few surprises. Rosa goes elsewhere for the unexpected.

Henry was still reading last night's paper with stern attention. When he and Rosalind are alone together he lays the paper flat on the table and reads it carefully as though it contained secrets which must be solved before he can leave the world unread until tomorrow.

Henry takes his news seriously, he is news-crammed. The more the world depresses him, the more careful attention he gives it, the more printed information he absorbs. He seldom reads books as he used to. He has forgotten how, though he does not realise this.

Rosa offers him toast. Old, worried and put upon by relatives, Henry is not the man he was. His skin is blotchy, his anger impotent and buried beneath the restraints of courtesy. If Henry were a Bedouin, he would give Bianca the sheep's eye.

'Bianca,' says Rosa, 'I have some business things to do in town. With Henry.'

She can hear herself saying it, her voice bright as a brass button rolling as she prattles on explaining the whereabouts of coffee, tea, kettles, the shaved ham in the fridge. 'You'll be all right on your own, won't you?'

'Of course,' says Bianca, her mind leaping to the glint of the retractable steel tape measure on the garage shelf, her outstretched hand disturbing cobwebs as she reaches. There are kitchen steps there too. 'Don't worry about me. And I'll clean up this mess.' She waves a hand over the checked tablecloth, the Shasta daisies, the crumbs.

'Thank you,' says Rosalind.

It would have been different if the baby had not died, Bianca knew that. She would have had looks, that stillborn child, how could she not. She would have married a fine man unscarred by financial collapse. Bianca saw her daughter, blonde, blue-eyed, holding out pale arms to embrace: Of course you must come to us, Mother. We wouldn't hear of anything else, would we . . . There was a gap, rather a tall gap. Angus? Hugh? He didn't have to be Scottish. But he was insistent, pressing, he was . . .

Bianca swept toast crumbs with an angry hand. What on earth are you thinking of, woman? Justin had called her 'woman'. It had been a private joke. She saw him in uniform, unexpectedly home for lunch. 'Where's m'woman?' he called from the hall and she ran laughing.

If the baby had lived it would have been 'women'. 'Women,' she said loudly and burst into tears, bitter, stupid, angry, gulping tears of no use to anyone, least of all herself.

Sniffling, snorting with self-disgust, she pulled herself up and cleared the table. She shook the cloth out the window, watched the birds lined up on those hideous telephone wires as they swooped to peck. She washed the dishes with plenty of nice hot soapy water, put on Rosa's plastic apron with mad chefs dancing and headed for the garage. She had plenty of time.

'Hi,' called a voice from the hall, 'anyone home?'

Bianca swayed, teetered on the top of the paint-spattered steps, her heart thudding. She steadied an arm against a wall and scrambled down. The retractable measure, dropped in fright, lay at her feet, its end thrashing like a steel snake. The shame, the shock, the . . .

A man stood in the doorway, his shape backed by light. 'What are you doing?'

What was she doing? What could she possibly be doing except gaping in fright at the shadowed figure smiling at the door. 'I, that is . . .' Anger saved her. 'It's more a question of what you're doing in my sister's house. Get out at once.'

The smile widened, filled the face with laughing disbelief. 'Good God, Auntie Bianca.' Rufus dropped his pack with a thud and held out his arms.

Bianca sat down suddenly on the arm of one of the chairs. It gave under her weight, rocked slightly. She had no breath, no breath at all.

'Rufus,' she panted. 'Why didn't you write to me?'

He dropped to his heels before her, took her hand. 'You're so right. Why didn't I? Why the hell didn't I? When I think how good you've been to me. The presents. That coat, remember the coat? I've still got it, good as new.' His eyes flicked, smiled again. 'Yes. You know the first present I remember you giving me? At Uncle Andy's funeral. A Dinky truck. Well, I was too young to remember but Mum told me, and I reminded you of it in Titchfield, remember? The Dinky truck when Uncle Andy died?

'I've still got all my Dinkys, collector's items now but I'm hanging on to them, boxes and all. They must go up. They'll be like Steiff bears one day. There's a lot of money in toys if they're in good condition. People don't realise. Most of them are shot to hell, of course, that's why.'

Bianca slid from the arm of the chair into its depths with uncharacteristic clumsiness. How could the cherubic child of that time, of subsequent photographs on a stool with one leg tucked beneath him and the other sticking out and curls as thick as Millais's *Bubbles*, have turned into this unusual-looking man. She had not seen him for years, since he had gone home from the UK the first time and Justin's long decline into dementia had begun. She looked at him carefully. In fact he had not changed, not even from the early photographs. He had merely expanded, stretched and enlarged in all directions. He still looked well fed, his curls still rioted.

Rosa had tried with the hair when he was young. Photographs throughout the years had demonstrated the close crop (I'd hide the skinhead if I were you, darling. Justin.), the semi-sheer, the mop. Nature had burst through them all. *All the boys look quaint at the moment*, wrote Rosa on the back of a pre-Raphaelite maiden astride his new bike, *and Henry says there are worse things than long hair.*

The hair now hung in curls the colour of pine shavings streaked with gold. His eyes were the unclouded blue of a sparrow's egg.

He was still smiling as he picked up the tape measure; a reserved smile, a what's-going-on-here smile. 'And what were you doing, Aunt?'

He had remembered her dislike of auntie. That was something.

'Justin died,' she said. 'Last year.'

'Oh my God.' He was beside her, hugging her, his muscles taut against her, enclosing her distress with strong-armed comfort. 'How terrible! And to think I didn't even know.'

'But why didn't you know?' she asked through tears. 'He had been ill for so long. Didn't your mother, didn't anyone . . . How could you not know?'

'Well, like I said, you lose touch. But with some people you have this conviction that when you meet up again it'll be just the same, and it's true. I hate not knowing about Justin, a fine man, a good guy, tragic . . . What a loss.'

Bianca shook her head. She was an honest woman. 'Not at the end. Not at the end at all, Rufus.'

Rufus, his arms still around her, kissed her.

He was now lying in the chair opposite her with his legs draped over one arm. 'You may call me Bianca if you like, Rufus.'

Rufus adjusted a cushion behind his head, considered. 'Bianca. It doesn't exactly trip off the tongue, does it? I'll call you Bee, if we've dropped the aunt thing.'

She opened her mouth to tell him that no he would not, that Bianca was a beautiful name, that . . . But he was so relaxed, his smile so friendly among the faded colours, the quiet streets of home. Leafy Meadowbank, Henry called it, but you never knew with Henry.

'So what's with the tape measure, Bee?'

She could tell him, she knew she could tell him. Rufus would understand. There was nothing shameful about taking measurements in a sister's house—nephew and aunt would laugh about it together, he would hold the end of the tape thing, no, he would be better up the steps. There was nothing furtive about the operation, nothing furtive about anything. *There is nothing*, she remembered, *either good or bad, but thinking makes it so*.

She laughed aloud, more cheerful than she had been since the day the Boeing had landed and every man, woman and dog at the Auckland airport had instructed her to have a nice day and her heart dragging like a lead balloon even before the plane doors had opened.

'I was doing some measurement—my things.'

The blue denim leg stopped swinging. 'Things?'

'Yes, I have a container of my things arriving any day. I was wondering where they would fit.'

Silence. Quite a long silence. Bianca's hand rose to her throat.

'Antiques?'

'If you call them that.'

'What do you call them?'

Bianca gave a little puff of mirth to show life was fun. Rufus did not respond.

'What about Mum's things?'

Bianca looked around the comfortable unco-ordinated muddle—the three-legged stools and sticks of furniture, the rags and patches were not things and never had been. That cushion, for example, that extraordinary cushion behind Rufus's head. It had red-capped elves on it, large canvas-work elves; someone had given them golden cricket bats, had stitched them and bound them and rested heads against them for a thousand years.

'Oh, Ros will be delighted,' she said.

Rufus was inspecting a dirty white shoe. His gaze was concentrated, his mind busy. He wouldn't bet on it.

'Tell me,' he said. 'Remind me about your things.'

Bianca did so. She told him of bun-footed coffers, of old rugs and rat-tailed spoons and . . .

Rufus was now upright, one foot touching the kitchen steps. 'So why were you up the wall when I came in?'

Bianca's blush took her by surprise. 'The longcase clock,' she murmured.

'Ah, the grandaddy. I like old clocks. I'll realign it, get it going for you.'

'Oh, I don't think . . .'

'I'm an expert. As long as it's genuine, of course. The old ones' mechanisms are a breeze.'

Bianca opened her mouth in protest and shut it. What on earth was he doing now. Rufus continued unbuckling the heavy bronze buckle of his belt and pulling it from its denim loops, his face stern as a puritan father's about to thrash his child for the sake of its soul.

He retucked his shirt, laughed his rueful laugh and smiled into her eyes. 'Something binding a bit.' He juggled, re-threaded, rebuckled. 'By the way, where are the olds? Dad's at the office, yeah. But where's Mum?'

'She had some business to do in town,' murmured Bianca, dragging her mind back from Titchfield when she and Justin were first married. Justin's brisk hands tugging at corduroys, his head ducking oak beams. The Tippetts had asked them in for a drink. 'The Titchfield Tippetts with the floy doy,' Justin had called them. And where were the Tippetts now? Gone. Gone. No floy doy, no floy doy ever again and who cared what in heaven's name it meant or ever had. It meant shared jokes and long twilights and Justin's legs like pillars against the light.

They had made their excuses to the Tippetts. Goodness knows what they had said.

And here was this ape, this retarded ape dropping his trousers a yard in front of her nose.

'For heaven's sake, Rufus, surely someone has told you not to take off your trousers in public.'

'Well, I'd have said more "dropped", wouldn't you? An old battleaxe in the VD clinic, well it was then, used to say that. "Drop y'tweeds," she'd yell. She'd be shot now, of course. Things were much rougher in those days.'

Bianca's head was spinning. No, that was ridiculous. Her head was not spinning. Her head was angry. Uncouth, unmannered, loutish, he had got worse, much worse. 'How on earth do you know?'

'I used to work there.'

'As?'

'Medical orderly.' He was sitting opposite her once more, his hands clasped, his eyes kinder than ever, his hair shining. 'You're quite right, Bee. That was a crass thing to do. Inex-cusable. You get into bad habits living alone, don't you?'

'No.'

Rufus sighed, stared sadly into a corner of the room where sunlight was fading pale cushions paler. 'No,' he said, 'perhaps not.' He sat silent for some time then leapt up. 'Okay, Bee. Let's get the show on the road, get the measuring done. Where's your list?'

They worked happily, amicably. He was competent, supple, dropping onto his heels then rolling upright. He ran up and down the steps without looking, he jumped from the top and landed without a sound. He was nimble and measured quickly, he double-checked each figure. His grace, his agility, his competence reassured her. All she had to do was hold one end of the tape. He shot it along to her behind a sofa as they knelt at either end. She missed it and it shot back to him like an electric hare. They sat back on their haunches and laughed. It was fun.

'It'll be a tight squeeze, Bee,' he said finally, 'but you'll make it.' He rubbed a dirty shoe on the threadbare carpet. 'Lucky the carpet's so worn, the rugs won't canter all over the place. That'll be a help.' He walked around the room in silence, his hands in his pockets, his mouth pursed as he looked at the ceiling, ran a hand over the mantelpiece, walked into the hall. She heard a door open, close. He came back more thoughtful than ever, dropped to examine the deep skirting board and sprang up again.

'You could make money on this place, you know that? Rip out the furniture, lock stock and barrel, get shot of it. Stain the floors throughout, rush through with a lick of paint. People in their forties, the guys with money, they're into colonial villas, heritage, all that. Any fool can slap in an en suite, but where are you going to get joinery like this nowadays? Look at these doors, look at them. Kauri. Unobtainable. Class stuff. This place could be a showplace, an absolute showplace.'

'This place?'

'Genuine kauri villa. Ask yourself. Not many round here. Good locality, schools, shops, bus route. Tart up the garden. Cottagey—hollyhocks, roses, what are those little things that smell?'

'Pinks,' said Bianca faintly, one hand on the back of a chair.

Rufus snapped his fingers, ran a hand down an architrave. It was a small hand for a man, the fingers stubby and not entirely clean. A boy's hand. 'Pinks,' he said.

'You said, you said you could make money,' said Bianca staring into his eyes. They seemed to have lightened.

'So you could, no doubt about that.'

'But what about my things?'

The pause was infinitesimal, over before her mouth had closed.

'Hang on. I've got an idea. Sit down and I'll tell you.'

His idea was ridiculous, insane, not to be countenanced for a second.

'Bed and *Breakfast*. Why in the name of all that's merciful would I want to run a Bed and Breakfast?'

'Because you haven't any money.'

Bianca was shaking with rage, her face and neck mottled. They went blotchy with anger, shamed her more. 'How dare you say that!' Who had told him. Not Ros, surely not Ros. 'How do you know?' she whispered.

'Why else would you come home?'

'Home?'

'Back then. I've seen it before. People with no cash always come home. Or old age. You need a few rellies when you start packing up.'

Bianca laughed. How could she not laugh at this idiot, this child with nous, this astonishing nephew.

Rufus hugged her again. It was a long time since Bianca had been hugged with conviction.

'Now calm down, Bee, calm down,' he said. 'You've got it all wrong about Bed and Breakfasts. The B and B scene's changed completely. It's a fun thing now. There's a heritage input from people with fully restored colonials, decos, old barns out in the bush, squattocracy, the lot. I could rip through this place in a flash; four good-sized double bedrooms, triple, a couple of them. Put in a mini en suite. Then we put in your antiques. Can you imagine? Well, you can better than me, but I can remember a lot.'

He was now springing about the room on his toes like an excited child. 'Can't you just see them?'

Bianca could, very clearly. She could see her things; their limpid patina, the gleam of centuries bestowed upon them by the work of others, the rose and apricot rugs, the rosewood commode, the Meissen parrot. And people would see them, people would admire, ask her about them, get her to explain about stringing and inlay and things she knew about. Ros and Henry, she knew, would never even look at her things, much less appreciate them.

She could see Americans, courteous men in pastel jackets with sharp-eyed wives twittering, 'Isn't this darling, Arthur? See, it opens in back.'

Bianca sat straighter. 'What about Breakfasts?'

'Continental. No sweat. Put out a few cereals, fruit, toast and you're in business. You don't have to make a feature. Some do a full English but it's up to you.'

'I wouldn't want children.'

'*No pets. Unsuitable for children. No smoking*. Just put it in the brochure.'

They sat together side by side, their faces intent as children staking their claim for a hut in the lupins. They were united.

*

Rosalind was exhausted and ashamed. Emotion is draining, they say, but which one? Where does shame fit?

She sat silent beside Henry as he drove home through the Domain, her over-full bag clutched on her lap, her eyes wide as they searched the rough area of the gully to the left. It was verdant, that was the word, verdant and dappled and soothing to the eye, this place where a homeless vagrant had been murdered recently. A pleasant woman, apparently, known to local shopkeepers for her honesty. She had owned a house nearby originally and something had gone wrong and she had run out of money.

Rosalind's hands tightened as they swept through. It could never happen, not here in Parnell, and it had. It could happen to Bianca. But would not because Bianca had her sister Ros and her sister's kind husband Henry. Ros who had sneaked out of her house leaving her sister among toast crumbs so she could go to the city and plot against her.

Which had proved a fatiguing and unproductive exercise. Rosalind had sat all morning at Felton Fabric Importers in the small vacant office which was used only occasionally by a temp when the workload on Lorraine became unacceptable. Many things were unacceptable to Lorraine, from outmoded computers to all this fuss about land claims.

The back office had been occupied by Martin Brown, a war veteran Henry had insisted on employing despite increasing infirmities caused by mortar fire. Martin, as he told Rosa, had left half his innards at Cassino. 'Never seen hide nor hair of them since.' He had been declared fit in time to be captured at the Senio, and had learned what he called survival Italian, which had been useful in the firm. He had established contacts, had gone on some of the buying trips with Henry and been invaluable.

The survival joke was typical of the man. He picked up words and examined them as Rosalind did. She saw him through the years, his feet splayed wide and purposeful as a penguin's as he came to greet her, '*Ciao, bella.*' They became friends, unlikely well-tempered friends, and remained so long after the effects of Cassino had caught up with him and he had retired to a council rest home in Takapuna where he lies on his bed and smokes. Meals on Wheels are a lifesaver. He doesn't know what he'd do without his Special Bland Reduction Fruit, he tells Rosa as they crack the crossword together and find that the answer to *Jones takes the plunge* is *Inigo*, and are pleased.

Someone from the RSA visits him, and always on Anzac Day. People are kind, you wouldn't believe.

There is a desk in Martin Brown's ex office, a chair, a *Great Gardens of Italy* calendar and a telephone. The calendar is in Italian and continues to be sent every year by one of his former contacts. Henry offers them to their recipient each year but Martin says that although it is a kind thought he needs a calendar like a hole in the head, so Henry continues to hang the thing in the back office. Why, he does not know. Apart from anything else, it is in Italian. Easy enough to work out because *domenica* is in red but why bother.

Rosalind stares at the calendar for a long time. It occurs to her that they might be running out of Great Gardens of Italy but this does not appear to be so. The photo angles in the Villa d'Este seem infinite and may need to be if the series goes on much longer. She looks for gardens near Milan.

Rosalind works her way through Real Estate Agents from Access to Wyatt. Do you have a letting agency? she asks. No or Yes. In what area? Unfurnished? Yes. And the price per week? Oh dear.

The prices for flats, apartments, let alone townhouses or designer units with dip pools have gone, you could say, through the roof. Henry was right. It is impossible. Rosalind touches a red *domenica*. Nothing is impossible, but she is undoubtedly out of touch with rents.

Her last experience was nearly twenty years ago when Rufus had been studying law. He had not wanted to live at home; what student did in the days before the grants were slashed.

She had ignored the obscene graffiti on the wall of old houses in the deep-litter flats he had shared, had resisted the impulse to clean up, had walked past open doors and the crumpled bed of entwined male flatmates. We all take our pleasures differently, as Henry said, and she agreed. Nevertheless the first glimpse of two unshaven faces on the same pillow and the dirty coffee mugs alongside had startled her. Mind you, it had been early in the morning. She had been taking Rufus out to Pukekohe to see Granny Felton, who liked to get her visitors over early so she could get on.

Henry put his arms around her when she told him later, kissed the top of her hat.

'It's just culture shock. Forget it.'

'And the love bites. His neck's black and blue.'

'Any fool can bite a neck.'

True. Gone were the polo-necked jerseys, the bandages, the sticking plasters of their youth. Love bites were now proud trophies displayed like sabre cuts. As was pregnancy and so it should be, how else. But the vast profferings of pregnant bellies above bikini pants had confused her at first.

They walked slowly up the path to the house. Rosalind, her mind full of land agents, remembered that one of them had told her years ago that their home had street appeal. The man, his moustache eager, his hands juggling mythical sales, had assured her that this was of the greatest importance to would-be buyers. 'You want your house to sit up and beg,' he explained.

Which depressed her further. What street appeal their

house had once owned had been diminished by lack of attention to detail. The windowsills were flaking, the garden was in need of care and attention. Nature had encroached as it does in Auckland, control had not been maintained. The banana passionfruit had gone mad, tumbling over the white trumpets of the datura and heading for the pawpaws by the verandah. The curved path to the front door was overgrown, the buried treasures of its borders invisible.

She had become careless about the garden. And Henry had never been tempted to be otherwise.

He ambled along beside her, irritated both by her thinking for one moment that her hare-brained scheme could work and by the fact that she had not pulled it off. Had not produced the bijou flat from the hat for a song.

And some clown had parked a rusting Skoda too near the blind corner. And Bianca would be there and damn and blast and bloody hell.

She sat on the sofa, her pretty feet extended, laughing into his son's eyes.

Rosalind dropped her bag and ran. 'Rufus! Why didn't you let us know the day!' Arms around him, she was hugging, laughing, being swept off her feet.

Henry, his arms hanging, watched in silence. The words, the actions, but especially, oh especially the words of Rufus's home-comings had not varied in nearly twenty years. He put out his hand as he had done countless times, felt the same sensation of love plus the niggling guilt of dismay. He dropped the outstretched hand and embraced his son, banged his back like a veteran team-mate acknowledging a superb try from the new kid.

'Welcome home, boy, welcome home.'

There was a chortle from the sofa. No other word for it. Bianca had chortled. 'Boy,' she laughed. 'Some boy!'

Henry looked at her in silence.

'Wait till we tell you! Rufus and I have had the most marvellous idea.'

Rufus stirred. 'Now hang on, Bee, I'll . . . just . . .'

Rosalind, now scrabbling in her bag, its open jaws yawning in her hand, looked up quickly. 'Bee?'

three

They sat side by side clutching gin. Rosalind lifted hers and sipped, imbibing liquid like a small wary bird.

Henry drank deep. Bianca had declined his suggestion that discussion of the plan wait until after the meal, until tomorrow, until glaciers flamed over and Rufus grew up.

Rufus, after his first startled 'Hang on, Bee', had been equally keen to impart the good news.

Henry watched him. Nothing had changed. His son's bright-eyed enthusiasm, his sharing of joy, his frank delight at new schemes practical or impractical, from the totally ludicrous to the worth investigating, remained untarnished.

Did the man think, in his wildest dreams, that his parents would countenance such insanity? Would have their home gutted, be cuckooed out of their warm muddled nest for some get-rich-quick scheme which would not work, and which, even if, against all possible odds, it did work, would be of no benefit to either of them, in fact quite the reverse. It was farcical, it was burlesque; but Henry, like Rosa beside him, knew from past experience that Rufus must be heard out.

He needed, as he had often told them, time to explain, to extrapolate, to reveal the wonders of future profits to his hearers.

If they refused to listen life became impossible. Rufus sulked, nagged, withheld affection and went dog on them. He behaved, thought Henry, like a spoiled coquette. The fun, the happiness he engendered seeped from the house, the horseplay dissipated, the singing in the shower dissolved itself into a dew.

Until they would listen, would sit through what he called his presentations, which became increasingly complicated throughout the years, presentations which involved computer printouts, pie diagrams and spreadsheets demonstrating wealth waiting to be accrued, Rufus would not play.

When they had given him a fair hearing and kept their faces straight (a skill Henry had sometimes found impossible, with disastrous results), then and only then would Rufus reward their patience. They were allowed to say what they thought of the plan in which he was inviting them to invest money.

When Henry said no, gloom descended on the house like a damp tarpaulin, but gradually, sometimes within twenty-four hours, Rufus would accept the situation and reappear, would be available for loving, would make life good once more.

It seemed, sometimes even to Henry, that this was fair enough. Henry made the living, Rufus contributed much that made the living worthwhile. Henry enjoyed his job, was knowledgable about fine fabrics and their purchase and marketing. His firm continued to make money despite increasing competition. Not as much, certainly, as in his father's day but how could it? He loved his son. Why not indulge? Support. Learn to overlook his own apprehension.

The only thing we have to fear is fear itself, said Franklin D Roosevelt and Henry agreed. And apprehension is not fear, apprehension is a taste in the mouth, a dryness, a doubt. Nothing more. Why not relax? Enjoy.

Because he couldn't. Because he was involved. Because the blood of generations of hard-working upright men and women pumping through his heart forbade it. He would not admit his fears, not to his inmost soul, wherever that was. He would not admit the questions, let alone the answers. Questions which lay stretched like faceless dogs guarding the entrance to his conscious mind. Had Rufus a moral sense? Did he know right from wrong? Did he care whether he knew or not? Was he one of those people about whom Henry has read, people in whom there is some aberration in the genes, something lacking in the building blocks of conscience. 'I want, therefore I take.'

Yet what in the name of Heaven did he fear? There had been no brush with the law, no incidents, no slippery slopes. Nothing untoward had occurred and never would and he must not worry Rosalind with his vague misgivings.

He had not tried to interest Rufus in his business in the downtown Auckland warehouse. Rufus, he assumed, was not warehouse material. He was the antithesis of Martin Brown, he despised routine. Rufus wanted real money, serious money he told them. He would get a law degree and branch out.

He dropped his law studies after eighteen months. Useless crap. Need their heads read, the lot of them. Not one of them had a clue. Not an entrepreneurial skill in sight. The whole ethos sucked.

Henry, his hand lying on Rosa's as though anchoring it to the nest of singing birds beneath, remembered Rufus's infancy. There are words now for the infinite variety of childhood; phrases such as attention deficit disorder and over-achiever and special abilities. Where were the words in the '60s for business-minded toddlers. Words such as entrepreneurial, streetwise, financially astute. Then Rufus had seemed merely disarmingly different, enchantingly so. Which other three-year-old liked the Fat Controller better than Thomas the Tank Engine. Could not understand why another one (Edward, the blue?) was happy to be back on his own little branch line after tasting life on the fast track.

He saw his son's naked back view, the pink legs pumping, the cherub buttocks tight with excitement as he ran to stow Granny's half-crown in his little 'ootcase'. The little suitcase featured large. Every treasure was guarded and stowed away; unwrapped sweets, unread books and best, oh best of all, his monies, were all stored in a fibre lunch case left over from Rosa's schooldays. His pennies became cents when he was seven years old, a process which interested him enormously. Where had they gone, the big brown ones? Why were there all these little ones? How were the little ones the same as the big ones when they weren't?

His suitcase went everywhere with him. Like all obsessionally loved items of childhood, it became a bore to his parents. Unlike some, it was never lost or mislaid.

Men or women of mild goodwill bent to ask Rufus what he was going to be when he grew up. He gazed up at them, his eyes rounder than ever. 'Rich,' he said. By the time he was ten he had decided to be a millionaire. He bred guinea pigs, kept accurate records of progeny and prices obtained. Perhaps out of habit he kept the records in the same battered brown case alongside those of his fish-breeding enterprises. Disaster struck the fish in the form of tail rot, but the guinea pigs sold well. He avoided pet shops. They were middlemen living on the profits of the workers.

He collected coins and stamps. He read deeply on his chosen subjects but the assets accrued too slowly. His schemes became more enterprising. He bought webbing belts from Army Surplus and kitted out his fourth form at considerable profit. The belts were declared non-uniform and banned, but by this time the money was banked and how could Rufus have known that old Benson would stuff things up. '*Caveat emptor*,' he told the puniest boy in the class and biked home from Grammar by different routes for a week or two. There is nothing cute about being dumb.

As far as his parents could see, he was happy at school; he passed exams, was friendly but not sociable. His schemes took up much of his time, he played a lone hand until the plan either succeeded, in which case why tell the bludgers, or failed, in which case why tell anyone. Rufus knew that greed was good long before the man wrote the book which told the world.

And yet it was not greed, thought Henry, enmeshed once more in the web of love and astonishment Rufus had engendered for the last twenty years before it dawned upon him that his son would not change. This blinding flash had enabled him to face facts. To tell Rosa in all honesty that Rufus would be all right. He did not mean, as he knew Rosa hoped, that Rufus would settle down, start paying income tax and breed babies with some shadowy devoted wife. Rosa had shown him a full-page advertisement recently from an English paper—one of those beautifully lit black and white ones of such perfection that you ignore the product advertised. Yoghurt? Designer underwear? A beautiful young man lay gleaming and naked on a beach, his eyes closed against the sun, a sleeping infant draped along his torso.

'Nice?' she murmured.

'Rosa,' said Henry, and was silent. What could he say, what could he possibly say. Rufus is Rufus. He will be all right. He is Rufus. He is different. He is ours.

He was fifteen when he came bursting into his father's warehouse one day on his way from school.

He was onto a marvellous option.

'Option?'

He, Rufus, had a contact. A guy named Tod . . .

'One d or two?'

'Aw shit, Dad, one I think. What does it matter?'

'One d means death in German.'

His son's shoulders slumped. Henry tried again.

'Tell me. Tell me about Tod.'

Tod was onto a good thing. Why no one had thought of it before Rufus could not imagine. What Tod was onto, was into looking at, was about to tender for, was the franchise for distributing cigarette vending machines for hire in your own home. 'And we service them. Keep them stocked up and that. How about that!'

Henry laughed. He laughed till he wept. He lifted his eyes from his mopping handkerchief to his son's white face, to acne and pain.

'Sorry,' he gasped. 'It's just . . . it's just, why would anyone want such a thing in their house?'

Legs apart, toes poised for flight, Rufus socked it to him. 'For convenience, of course. Saves going to the dairy, you thicko.'

'And don't call me thicko.' Henry spoke without rancour. People who don't understand dreams are thickos, always have been and always will be. Why did I laugh? Because I am his father, because I got it wrong.

'Sit down, tell me about it,' he said, dragging a hand across his face. A cigarette vending machine in the privacy of your own home. It could be a talking point, a conversation piece, this tin box regurgitating fags when primed could become a source of mild envy.

Ah, I see you have one of those new Instafags.

The proud but modest, Yes.

Then what?

Henry pointed to a chair. 'Sit down,' he said again. 'Tell me all about it.'

That one was easy. Tod left town. Other schemes followed. Would Dad lend him the cash to do up that old shack down the road? No, Dad would not.

Why wouldn't they let him work on an oil rig? Because you're sitting School Certificate and they won't take you.

'What about my cash flow?'

'Stuff,' said Henry carefully, 'your cash flow.'

Guy I know organises parties for his mates, his auntie's got a garage. Gets the liquor in bulk, anything, he can get it. Knows a bloke, back-pocket deal. Wants me to go in fifty-fifty. Going like a bomb. They want more. Lots more.

There's money in Grey Power, Dad, you know that? Well, some. I'd rent the buses at first. Plough the profits back in. The sharp guys are just waking up to the transport angle, old guys like being driven. Bus travel's a whole new scene now. Completely upmarket, none of those rough rides and kids tossing down your neck. Air-conditioned, huge windows, sheepskins, they lap it up. Gardens, little tootles, wineries, seafood restaurants, shopping trips, you name it, they're on.

Guy I know made a packet out of *Jesus Christ Superstar*.

Rufus left for his OE in '78. He had spent the time since dropping out of law organising a student co-operative of house painters. They were a cheerful crew; quick, efficient and cleaned up well. Their prices were reasonable, or seemed so to Henry. Rufus interviewed the prospective clients, mostly old ladies. 'We're not professionals,' he told them, 'but we're keen and quick. And what's more we come when we say we'll come and we stay on the job. None of this here today gone tomorrow stuff, Mrs Wilkes. I can promise that.'

Oh, the relief. No more waiting, no waiting in day by day for professionals who said, 'Monday it is, Mrs Wilkes', and where were they.

'You know how you can tell a professional, Mrs Wilkes?'

Mrs Wilkes looked into the clear eyes and passed the vanilla cremes. 'No.'

Rufus was on his feet, one hand holding a phantom brush

as he demonstrated on the window frame. 'A professional can paint one sweep down here, and there won't be a single dribble on the masking tape. If he uses it, that is, and he won't. He doesn't need it. That's the difference.'

'But . . .' said Mrs Wilkes.

'Exactly. So why mention it?' Rufus gave a shy laugh. 'It doesn't matter, but that's the difference. You know about the maharajah who commissioned the Taj Mahal, Mrs Wilkes?'

Mrs Wilkes, uncertain but anxious to help, had heard something, but she didn't know it had been, as it were, commissioned.

Rufus's hands clapped together. 'Same difference. For his wife it was, in memory of his dead wife. The architect that the maharajah chose, you know what his plan, his submission for the job was?'

Mrs Wilkes shook her head, though there was something in the back of her mind she would like to have shared with this friendly young man. Something to show that she knew and had always known a great many things. That it was just that nowadays some of them disappeared when required, to click into her mind when it was too late and her fellow conversationalist had gone home. You could scarcely ring and tell them.

'Circle!' she said suddenly. 'He drew a circle.'

'Right first time. Not many of the ladies get that. Like you say, the architect just drew a circle, a perfect freehand pencil circle and the maharajah knew he was dealing with a pro.'

'Yes,' said Mrs Wilkes. 'But I've always wondered how. And what was your telephone number again, Rufus?'

There had been a cloud, a mist of dissension when Rufus dissolved the co-operative.

Terry and Mike and Jake and Lloyd no longer piled into the house at Meadowbank as they had done all through the summer. Mind if I have a shower, Mrs Felton? I smell like a goat. No, no, Jake, please do. Nimble, there and back in a flash, Rosa distributed towels, beer, food and loved every minute. She felt, that summer, like a multiple mother, a warm-hearted, competent figure offering nourishment to many.

The team liked her in return, they spared her embarrassing questions. Mike bailed up Henry as he was putting the car away.

'Mind if I have a word, Mr Felton? It's about the co-operative. Things seem to be a bit slow coming through, the wind-up payments. Do you happen to know when Roof's coming back?'

Henry stared at his key ring, rubbed the bronze F and waited.

Mike wiped his palms on his jeans. 'Can you tell us where he is?'

'With his grandmother in Pukekohe, the last time I heard.'

Mike pulled an envelope and a stub of pencil from the back pocket of his jeans. 'And the name?'

'Felton.' Thicko.

The sunburned face lifted. 'It could've been the other one. And the number?'

'Don't bother. I'll get on to him right away.'

'No worries. I'll give him a ring.'

'I have said I will deal with it, Michael.'

Henry heard his son's footsteps, the distinctive prancing stride. 'Rufus,' he called. 'Come here.'

'Where?'

'My office.' Which was a joke. The back verandah had been glassed in, a double-sided patchwork curtain designed by Rosa in her free-form period divided the area in two. Henry's side was made from more manly remnants, in colours suitable for a masculine workspace; greys, blues, woolshed reds and rusty browns hung beside a second-hand desk, old filing cabinets and two ten-dollar chairs. 'Why are they so cheap?' Henry had asked the man with the crew cut. 'Not good sellers this shape, I have to say. It's the legs.' The man laid a consoling hand on green leatherette. 'Very '50s, but a steal at this price.'

Rosa's end of the verandah was a riotous assembly of colour and mess. An ironing board sat beside an old-fashioned sewing machine crouched for instant action. Piles of treasured scraps, remnants and warehouse offcuts spilled from plastic bags or cartons on shelves alongside. A macramé plant holder containing a dead cactus hung from the ceiling beside an upside-down patchwork parrot. Something had gone wrong with the attachment to its wooden hoop and Rosa had never been a fixer; the fun was in the making. One day she would mend the thing so its proud yellow beak no longer drooped like an unused cutlass, one day she would finish her small hand-woven tapestry inspired by a 2000 BC Egyptian fish vase, one day she would replace the bobbles of her canvas-work cushion depicting bunches of square grapes. And what did it matter if she didn't. She had her own space which, she had read somewhere, was important and, what was more, so had Henry. And all because she had had the sense to run up a curtain.

The acid blues, sharp greens and stinging yellows of her side had startled Bianca. She put up a hand against the onslaught of colour, the jangle of bells. 'Ooh,' she said, '*oranges and lemons.*'

'I'm so glad you like it,' smiled Rosa.

'What is it?' said Rufus.

'Have a seat.'

Rufus slid into the other chair, then sprang to his feet rubbing the thighs beneath short denim shorts. 'Shit, this stuff's hot. Talk about *Blazing Saddles*. Why did you buy this crap?'

'Because it's cheap.'

'Look, can't I get it across to you, Dad . . .'

'Rufus, I don't want to start . . .'

But he was off again. Henry had heard it a thousand times. The stupidity, the sheer insanity of buying crud. How essential it was to go for quality stuff. Top of the range. Mug if you don't.

'You've got to think, Dad, use your loaf. Look at this rubbish. You could be sitting on an ergonomically designed Italian number, upmarket fabric, ball-bearing wheels, shoot all over the place like a dentist . . .'

Henry looked at his son in silence. Perhaps he was in some way, in some indefinable way, in need of help. And yet who or what could possibly change the mindset of this young thruster with entrepreneurial ambitions, or would want to. He saw his paternal grandmother, a sad, withdrawn woman whom he had never liked, looking sourly at his father's new Buick, his father in a snap-brimmed hat anxious beside her. 'Champagne tastes and ginger-beer income,' she sniffed.

'Rufus, Mike had a word with me yesterday. He said the rest of the gang haven't had their final payout.'

'Oh, that's all under control, Dad. No problems. Bit of a glitch at the moment . . .'

'Why?'

A quick impatient flick of the hand. 'You know how these things go.'

'No, I don't. Mike said it was equal whacks. That was what you all agreed. Tell me more. Explain.'

Rufus didn't, not exactly. After much circumlocution he told Henry that he was entitled to a major share because who got the thing up and running? Who chatted up the old ladies? None of it, not one bloody lick of paint would have happened without Rufus's enterprise and initiative.

Henry sat searching the face in front of him, watched the

eyes veiled by pale lashes. How could he explain to his son about honour, integrity, the word is the bond. Laertes had at least *hearkened* to his father, had given him a hearing. Henry and Rufus, like Sidney Smith's protagonists, would be arguing from different premises. From premises separated by oceans of incomprehension and seas of dissent.

He saw Rufus in glory at the Sunday School break-up, singing with the passionate conviction he gave to everything, his arms moving across, up, down in three-dimensional demonstration of his knowledge that his Redeemer lived and loved him.

Wide, wide, as the ocean
Deep, deep, as the sea.
High, high, as the heavens above
Is the Lord's love for me.

That there would be stars in his crown.

'Equal shares,' said Henry.

'Oh, all right, all right.' Rufus was on his feet, his hand clutching patchwork. 'You don't understand a bloody thing, you know that?'

'I know,' said Henry. 'I know that.'

Correspondence from overseas had been limited but this was to be expected. Rufus had never been what he called a paper man but he had a good eye for a postcard. He sent Rosa bare-breasted maidens gazing with *Wish you were here* on the back.

Henry smiled bleakly. 'I didn't know he was going to the Solomon Islands.'

'No,' said Rosa, still giggling. 'But he must have, mustn't he?'

'Presumably.'

Rufus sent shoes to Rosa. Elegant Thai silk shoes for Christmas, beautifully made Italian mules for her birthday. 'Why shoes?' asked Rosa, clutching a Bruno Magli to her bosom. 'They're lovely, but so expensive. And the postage. Besides, you know me.' She wriggled an aptly named Kumf for Henry's inspection.

Henry inspected the packing. 'Extraordinary-looking stamps,' he muttered.

Rufus rang collect from London. There was a killing to be made in rugs, especially Caucasians. And kilims, though that, of course, was a whole new ball game. They both went with the whole Habitat thing: clean lines, strong colours, nothing flowery. He'd been to see a guy in one of the big warehouses down at the docks. Acres of rugs, floor to ceiling, amazing. There are tricks to the trade. Not anything like chemical washing or phoney aging with scrubbing pumice or whatever, but they don't all have to be peed on by camels. The guy had contacts. They were going to join up, head off next month for Kirovabad. Small time at first but the future was looking good.

Henry sent the money. He heard no more. The postcards ceased, there were no more shoes, but Rufus rang occasionally.

Everything was 'good', that casual catch-all word which covers everything and tells nothing.

Even Bianca was good. You should see the stuff she's got. From top to bottom, from bottom to top. Good stuff. Very good. It's all Justin's, of course, but as far as she's concerned it's hers. Always banging on about her things, and besides the man's a real no-hoper. Not Bianca's fighting weight at all. He had refused to give Rufus his service greatcoat, even though he no longer wore the thing. Even the buttons would be worth a packet at his stall. Oh, hadn't he mentioned his stall. Down at the market.

'Which market?'

'The one near here.'

'Where's here?'

Bianca had bought him an overcoat which was kind but not the point of the deal. Bianca was very thick with a guy called Barry at the local antique shop. Nice guy, camp, very knowledgable. Good contact, very good. As was Aunt Bianca. All that stuff; a real eye-opener.

He followed Mrs Thatcher's career with interest, which surprised Henry, who had thought of him as apolitical. He called her Maggie without abhorrence. She reminded him in some ways, he said, of Aunt Bianca. Plenty of attack, straight shooter, knows where she's going, though Aunt Bianca won't go anywhere with that prick Justin. They're not unalike in looks, either, though of course Bianca's younger. He'd stayed a weekend with them recently. Terrible coffee and the smallest gin in the world. A gimlet, ever heard of a gimlet, Dad?

'No,' said Henry, smiling into the mouthpiece and shaking his head.

'Gin and neat Rose's lime juice. Neat. And God, the coffee. Do you reckon she puts salt in it?'

Henry was still nodding, nodding silently and lovingly through thousands of miles of ether to the fruit of his over-anxious loins. He laughed aloud.

'What is it?' yelled the voice.

'Quick, quick.' Rosa was at his elbow. 'It's my turn.'

Rufus had arrived home unannounced, unexpected and uncommunicative. Henry tried to find out how he had managed to exist for six years overseas, and not only to exist, but to make money. The answers were inconclusive and dismissive. Rosa tried when Henry was absent as she knew Henry, although devoted, was not interested in how his only child had managed to cope. Rufus would be all right.

Henry took his son to lunch at one of those cool, unobtrusive, downtown restaurants with a good wine list and men in suits. There was little laughter in their discussions. These were serious men.

As were Rufus and his father. Henry was not aware that his son owned a suit. Apart from his gilded hair, he melted into the background, was appreciative of the wine list and talked politics. He had come back, he said, as soon as he heard they'd got rid of Muldoon, floated the dollar and all that. Thank God for Labour. He had kept in touch. A guy he knew, New Zealander, had the financial guff sent over, has had for years. Now Lange and co. have taken over, the whole place'll open up, take off, the age of enterprise and initiative will begin and Rufus planned to be part of it. Buoyant economy, get-ahead attitudes, that's what we're looking at. New Zealand's the place to be in the '80s and Auckland's the place to be in New Zealand. No doubt about that.

His voice did not rise. His usual exuberance appeared dampened, he glanced over his shoulder occasionally. People don't believe me, he said. They think because I've been away for a few years I haven't a clue. Suits me. I've brought my money back and I'm ready to roll.

'How much money?'

'Enough.'

'What are you going to put it in?'

Rufus waved a hand.

'Have a word with Charlie Adamson,' said his father.

'That old dugout. He's still losing the Somme.'

'Wrong war. And for God's sake keep your head. The market's going mad. Keep clear of it.'

Rufus had made money, a lot of money. How else could he have lost so much so spectacularly on Monday, 19 October 1987?

Rosa rang Henry. He's just sitting here. He has been all day. People keep ringing him, every time it's worse. Oh,

Henry, I've never seen him like this before. He looks . . . I can't tell you what he looks like. It's all gone, everything. Every penny he had. Oh Henry, I told you. I told you I was worried.

Rufus departed overseas once more. His debts were not impossible. He had not been home long enough.

He came home several times during the next eight years. He was doing well. Business was thriving.

'What business?'

'Same racket as you, Dad, the rag trade. Kids' wear. Find a good design . . .'

'How do you mean find?'

'All right. Industrial espionage, if you must. The name of the game in the rag trade and always has been. Where've you been, Dad?

'Then off to the sweatshops of Asia, I presume?'

'Yeah. The main problem is continuity. Your contacts can fold on you. Whole workshops can disappear overnight.' But Rufus had got a reliable network set up at last. 'You have to watch them, of course. Talk about tough. Watch them like a laser. But you just have to take people as you find them. Everyone's different. Taiwan, ever been to Taiwan?'

'No.'

'My God, they put you through it there and not only as regards business. The entertainment, the stuff they produce for their honoured guests to eat. They're testing you, see; sheep's eyes have got nothing on it. I told you about live ducks' feet?'

'No.'

'And monkeys' brains? They bring them to the table live same as the ducks, slice the top of their skulls off and there's the raw brains sitting wiggling at you on the plate.'

Rosa left the room. She came back white-faced, beads of sweat on her upper lip and forehead.

'But you love animals,' she begged.

'I do. I always have, like you say. I nearly had a fight with a guy in the market. He had live snakes on poles, dozens of them writhing about. Just hack off a bit, hand it over, guy goes off munching. No way they'll allow photos, well, who would? So I told him I'd buy the lot and he went berserk. I had to run for it in the end.'

He looked sadly at his mother's censorious frown. 'What could I have done with them, I thought later? They weren't even whole, half of them.

'And the same in the restaurant. What did you expect me to do? What could I do. People are different. It was an honour, it was business.' Rufus leaned back on elves. 'I take people as I find them. You have to in business, don't you, Dad?'

Henry lifted his hand from his wife's. It rose as though release from pressure had buoyed it upwards. Rufus had not taken long to reveal the details of the newest plan. He and Bianca sat side by side, partners who understood and were grateful for the strengths of the other. Bianca's hand touched Rufus's arm occasionally. She liked plans and that was one thing about New Zealand, you can do the most extraordinary things and no one will care. Sometimes when she had been abroad with Justin, Rapallo say, or Portofino, Bianca had looked down dark streets, seen gaiety, young men smoking and angry, dark-eyed girls. 'Let's go down there.'

'For God's sake, Bianca, don't be so Mrs Wentworth Brewster.'

And she had laughed at his wit and they had walked back to the Hotel Miramar and the limpid beauty of the harbour below the balcony where they drank coffee. One drinks a lot of coffee abroad.

While in England, Bianca had missed her enjoyment of hard physical work. Idleness did not come easily to her and she disliked golf and bridge. What she was good at was the hacking, taming, slashing type of gardening which she had practised in her mother's garden in Auckland, where growth has to be tamed not cosseted, where sub-tropical lianes threaten to strangle, where old roses go mad and leap down gullies, where Schiaparelli pink passion flowers do not astound. Titchfield gardens do not need to be tamed. Even walks in Hampshire are tamed. Bianca could understand her friend Linda, who had married a farmer thirty miles in from Otorohanga, a man who later left her for another woman. She missed him, of course, she told Bianca, but more than that she missed the farm. Not the beauty so much as the life, the satisfaction, the visible rewards of physical effort; the yards emptied, the shearing ended and their work done. Linda retreated to Otorohanga and pined for a life of vigour.

And now, especially now, now as never before, Bianca needed a project, something to absorb her completely.

Happiness, she had read somewhere, *is a by-product of absorption.*

Bianca thought about it, let it sink in, saw herself in an overall (Ros would have one), her hair tied up in a bandanna (Ros again), stripping, scrubbing, achieving happiness as a by-product of absorption.

She smiled at Rufus, patted his arm.

'I will tell you right now, Rufus,' said Henry, 'neither your mother nor I would countenance this idiotic scheme for one moment. As you must surely have realised.'

Rufus said nothing.

Bianca stared at him in panic. Her things, her Pembroke table, her Davenport, her longcase clock, all were disappearing from their appointed places in the room around her. Her scheme, her new life was collapsing before her eyes. She looked at Rufus's inert form, begged his idle hands.

'But you said, Rufus, you said.'

Rufus rose to his feet and stretched, dropped his palms behind his neck and yawned. 'Just an idea, Bee, just an idea. After all,' he explained, 'it's not our house, is it? Yours or mine.'

four

'How would you feel,' asked Rosa, 'if I asked you to come with me to see Martin Brown?'

Rufus glanced briefly from the real estate pages. 'Trapped. Where's Webster Street?'

'Why?' said Bianca, licking her spoon.

'Saturdays, the weekends generally, are so boring for him. He'd love to see you.'

'There's a unit for sale there.'

Henry rose stiff-legged and pompous. 'I'd be glad if you'd bring the paper to my office, Rufus. When you've finished with it, of course.'

'I don't want a unit! I want a villa, Rufus, like you said. To do up.'

'Take the damn thing, Dad.'

Bianca intercepted the transfer, gave a practised flip and scan. 'Look. Here's another one in Webster Street. *Wanted. Home handyman and TLC to restore this little gem. Great investment in desirable area.* What's TLC?'

'Please may I have my paper?'

'Tender loving care. It means it's a dump.'

'But look at the picture.'

Rufus peered over his aunt's shoulder at a smudged grey

cottage almost submerged beneath wisteria. A straight path led to the door. There was a hollyhock.

'Give me my paper!'

Bianca's smile was tender. 'In a moment, Henry.'

My heart is lurching. I must keep calm. This woman could kill me. Bianca, you seem unable to understand. What can I do to make you understand? We do not propose to hand our house over to you. We do not propose to buy one for you. There is no cottage. No house. Nothing. Nix. 'Thank you,' he said and took the paper.

Bianca sat motionless, one hand brushing imaginary crumbs from the swell of her bosom. She had had an idea.

'Rufus, are you coming with me to see Martin or not?'

'I didn't like the look of the weatherboards.' Rufus glanced in surprise at the ruffled bantam beside him. 'Sure, Mum, we'll go in Gaby's Skoda.'

Henry turned at the doorway. 'Is that the heap on the blind corner?'

'Yeah. Unless there's two.'

'Who's Gaby?'

'Aw, come on, Mum, I've told you about Gaby.'

'Never.'

'Gaby,' said Bianca faintly.

'Gaby's my partner.'

'Business or sleeping?'

'Both. And I don't like your tone, Dad.'

'I apologise.'

'Like hell you do. I would have you know . . .' Rufus was striding about the room, springing from his toes. 'I would have you know that if it hadn't been for Gaby I wouldn't be here today. I'd be dead. You're talking about the woman who carried me, bloody well half carried me, down from Poon Hill.'

'Where?'

'Near Annapurna. I was dead, half dead with Delhi belly. My pack, her pack, the lot. I could hardly crawl. I won't have you patronising Gaby.'

'Nobody's patronising anyone,' cried Rosalind. 'It's just that we didn't know about Gaby, did we, Henry?'

Henry shook his head. 'Or Poon Hill.'

'We want to meet her, we must meet her, thank her, everything . . .' She held out her hands. 'Oh Rufus, how are we to know things if you don't tell us?'

'Gaby,' said Bianca.

'I did tell you.'

'Never, never. Did he, Henry?'

'No.'

More silence. Rufus stopped prancing. Bianca stood up and sat down.

'Where is she now?' said Rosa finally.

'Matamata. There's a family wedding.'

'Why didn't you go?'

Rufus opened his arms. 'Because I wanted to get back to you guys. And besides, Gaby wasn't sure the Skoda would make it. It's been with her ex de facto while she's been away. The guy's just let it fall to pieces.'

Rosalind stood very straight, her head high. 'Will it get to Takapuna?'

'Oh hell yes. No sweat.'

'Good,' said his mother. 'Good.'

'Well, that's just as well,' said Henry, 'because I need the Sentra.'

'Why?'

'It's time I went to see Granny.'

Did I invent that, did I dredge up my aged old mother. I could scarcely invent her at this stage, but did I summon her up as a bolt-hole, an oh-my-God-let's-get-out-of-here escape.

An escape to the small cottage and green paddocks amid

encroaching ten-acre blocks and murmurs of motorway extensions, to the peace of well-sheltered orchards and his geriatric, alternative-lifestyle mother. Mrs Felton had moved out to Pukekohe when his father died. She had refused to budge, which was a worry, but her independence had its advantages. What if she had been as dependent as Bianca, had regarded her next of kin as safety nets and money as something which other people gave her smiling. Granny F had insisted on choosing her own ice-floe to head out to sea. She was captain of her soul, she took no orders. She was a cause for concern and it was high time he went to see her. Besides, he liked the tough old boot, enjoyed her company. There's no law against it.

Bianca leaned forward. She seemed incapable of asking a question without physical commitment, without being engaged. 'May I come too, Henry?'

Henry gaped at her. Here, offering her unwanted company, was the woman who, half an hour ago, had attempted to engage his son in a hare-brained collusion over a dead cottage in need of tender loving care plus a great deal of work and considerable money. He wanted to grab her by her plump shoulders, to shake her till she rattled. There is no money. You have none because your husband lost it. I will not give you mine which will later be Rosa's and eventually, God help us, our son's.

'Why?' he said eventually. 'Why on earth do you want to see her?'

'I don't want to see your mother particularly,' said Bianca, her mind elsewhere, 'but I'd like a run in the country.'

She must keep track of that advertisement, get some time to herself to cut it out before they left for Pukekohe and it was thrown away. Then work out exactly what she wished to say to Henry. Make notes to remind. There probably would be no need to consult them, just knowing they were there would be enough. Julian had been a great believer in notes. They clear the mind, he said, and there was much at stake.

'And then I'll answer my English Christmas cards when we get back,' she said, brushing again. 'You realise surface mail from here arrives about November 6th?'

'No,' gasped Henry. 'No, I hadn't realised that. Had you, Rosa?'

Rosa nodded. Bianca had complained for years of the penny-pinching habits of antipodean well-wishers. But Henry, who had scarcely glanced at a Christmas card in his life, was stretching out to her, seeking connubial support. She put an arm around him, patted his shoulder. 'You do now,' she said.

Rosalind sat high-rumped to help as the Skoda toiled up the harbour bridge. Rufus was telling her how much he liked his aunt, always had. 'Sure, she's got her weird bits but living with Justin wouldn't help. I got him a new toilet suite once . . . they were gussying up the downstairs lavatory.'

'Why you?'

'I knew a guy, got him a good price. They've all got really gross names: Regal, Royale, Consort. He ended up saying, "Very well, Rufus, if you can't get the Sovereign, I'm quite prepared to make do with the Regent."' Rufus gave a loud laugh, startling a gull from the girder alongside. It disappeared, hurtling downwards to the flat blue sea below. There was not enough wind for the yachts. They hung motionless between sea and sky, dependent on forces of nature.

'And when do we meet Gaby?'

'Gaby? Oh, any day now.'

The wanting to ask how things are with your offspring when you're not told, how they are *faring*, is like having a pool of liquid somewhere inside. It is not pathological, this fluid, neither is it essential like the pulsing thump of blood which knows where it's going and gets on with it, or the ordered bump and slosh of digestive processes. The pool of longing lies still, a mirrorless lake somewhere above the midriff. It comes and goes. It can be drained by answers.

'Tell me about her.'

'Well, you'll meet soon.'

'Yes, but tell me about her.'

'God, the North Shore's taken off, hasn't it?'

'No, it hasn't. Not Lake Road. It's just the same as always, only worse.'

'Looks okay to me.'

'It always was okay. It's worse now because there's more traffic.'

'Have it your way.'

She could have hit him. She very nearly did hit him.

He stroked the Skoda's rump as they arrived at the Sunnydale Rest Home. Something was on his side if not his inquisitive old bat of a mother.

The smell of nicotine in the small room was overpowering. Martin Brown lay on the bed, his yellow face and arms backed by tartan. He looked as though he had been thrown there. *Unregarded age in corners thrown*, thought Rosa, and wished she hadn't.

His walking frame was to hand for assistance to the bathroom straight ahead. The lavatory lid was raised, its all-seeing blankness stared back at them.

To the right of the bathroom door a huge television was operating full bore. Oprah Winfrey was being instructed by a young woman in pink tights and lip gloss how to make her Easter decorations for next to nothing. Oprah seemed interested, the young woman frenetic, as she cut, pasted and cut again; ribbons, tinsel, sequins, shiny paper and plain were all essential. Plus, of course, Oprah's own personal creative identity which every one of you guys out there has as well once it kicks in, is, like, you know, tapped. Isn't that right, Oprah? Oprah, staring at the small, complicated, yellow and green construction in her hand, agreed. Merlita was so right.

'Turn it off,' shouted Martin. 'Good to see you. Good. Good. Sit down.'

Rosalind kissed his pleated cheek and handed over a carton of cigarettes.

'I'll undo it for you,' said Rufus.

Martin handed him a packet.

'Thanks a lot.'

'I tried being an other-people's-only smoker myself,' said Martin, coughing, wheezing, killing himself but what the hell, 'but I wasn't getting enough. Be worse now, my word. Pariah dog country for smokers out there. Thank you, Rosa, thank you. So you're home again then.' He looked at Rufus, searching for clues as he had always done. He liked the man as he had liked the small boy. Rufus had made him laugh, he told a good story and had done from the age of four. Not all kids like talking to adults. Rufus had been happy to yarn for hours.

Martin saw the small brown hand on the lid of Tess's tin box labelled *Odds & Ends*, the drawer slipping shut as Rufus turned. 'I was just putting it back, Mr Brown,' he explained. 'I came in to talk to Tess and she wasn't here, and I saw this fifty cents on her desk and I thought hang and I was just putting it back.'

He had been a lovely kid.

'You'll come for lunch on your birthday, won't you, Martin?' said Rosa.

Martin looked at his friend. She attracted what you could call contact. She wished the world well and was disturbed by its conflicting interests. The rain would please the farmers but wasn't it bad luck for the school fête. It's hard to make money outside in the rain.

'Make up your mind, Rosa,' he had told her twenty years ago.

And here she was still trying. Wanting him to come, half dead and coughing his head off, to meet the po-faced sister whom he remembered with distaste, and these things are reciprocal.

'What about your sister, Rosa?'

'Oh, Bianca would love to see you again. Besides, it's her birthday as well.'

Bianca. What a name. Martin's eyes met Rufus's, flicked away quickly.

'Well, it's day by day these days, Rosa,' he wheezed. 'Very kind indeed, but that's months away, we'll have to see.'

'Take a raincheck,' said Rufus slipping another Rothmans from his pack. He had his own matches.

Martin stroked his tartan rug. It was a pity the boy's here, but why fuss. He couldn't ask him to clear out while he talked to his mother.

There's a lot of bull talked about love. Cherish is better. Rosa is cherishable and has been from the first moment I met her.

'I think I've got it all wrong, Mr Brown,' she whispered to him at her first office party after matrimony. The firm had been larger and more profitable then, and Mr Felton senior, despite his fears for the world as he knew it, had liked a good shindig. Rosalind glanced around the hot fug of the Christmas party, the slink of oyster satin bottoms gliding by, the proffered cleavage or two, the gaiety of converse. 'Wearing a sunfrock. I mean, look at them.' She flipped a finger beneath her nose, declined a fish ball. 'What the hell. Tell me, what do you do here?'

*

'Rosa,' he said, 'when I fall off the perch I want you to have what's left.'

Rosa had helped Martin with his banking for years and knew the pitiable state of his bank balance. But still. 'No, no, Martin, I wouldn't dream of it. What about your charities—RSA, Salvation Army?'

'You're my charity, Rosa. All my holdings, equities, the lot, all salted away. You'll be so rich you can leave what you like to the other buggers—or better still, blow the lot. Fat cat Rosa.'

Rufus was on his feet, his face serious. 'I don't want to intrude on this conversation. I don't think I should. No, no. I'll wait outside,' he said and disappeared.

Rosa looked at the old man in dismay. 'What on earth did you say that for? Rufus . . .'

You cannot say to a half-dead compulsive smoker, even if he is your best friend and you trust him, you cannot say, My son is interested in money and he might not realise you are joking.

She gave up, touched his stained hand briefly and picked up the crossword. '*Soldier ants remark to a friend*?'

Martin finished his cough and lay exhausted. '*Passant*,' he gasped.

Bianca was biding her time. She was wary of Henry and there was no hurry. It would be better to broach the subject on the way home.

'I had the most extraordinary dream last night,' she said.

Henry turned onto the motorway in silence.

'Princess Margaret was worried about her committee work. She was wearing rather a nice little hat, like half a stove-pipe with a feather. One of those practically all stalk ones with a little black fluff at the end. I was surprised, really, she doesn't often wear a hat indoors, let alone black. She asked me how I managed. "Well ma'am," I said, "in my experience, it all comes from the top. If the chairman is enthusiastic then she engenders enthusiasm in the whole of her committee. Unless you have a hard-working, enthusiastic—" Watch that lorry!'

'Truck.'

'It could have killed us. But it was odd, wasn't it? I mean dreams are of course, but this one was so real. She was very grateful and a footman arrived with tea and . . .' Bianca sat silent for a moment. 'It was funny it was Princess Margaret though, wasn't it? I mean . . .'

The asphalt ribbons of the motorway streamed southwards. A van labelled *Pandas of the Secret Dragon* passed too close. There was not much traffic.

He would understand, wouldn't he, if Bianca didn't come in to see Mrs Felton. Bianca was sure his mother would much prefer to see him alone. 'She probably scarcely remembers me.'

'Oh, yes, she does.'

Well even so, Bianca would be quite happy. She had brought the morning paper and the countryside is so pretty at this time of year. She might go for a little walk, though of course you can't walk here like you can in Hampshire. Lorries hurtling about all over the place.

She didn't walk. She checked her notes and reread the advertisement for the home handyman's dream and thought how she would make her point.

'And how was your mother?'

'Very well. She'd just killed a turkey for Easter. She gets very cross when they won't lie still.'

Typical. 'Did she mind my not coming in?'

'Not at all.'

Bianca glanced at him sharply. 'She never liked me.'

'No.'

'Does she still blame me for Andrew's death?'

'I didn't ask her.'

It is very peaceful near Pukekohe. Small green hills rise and fall, shelter belts grow tall, cows bellow but not often.

The time had come. 'Henry, I have something to tell you. I wonder if you would like to pull in to the verge and stop while I do so.'

Henry's idiotic eyebrows leapt high.

'For heaven's sake, woman, what can you say that would stop me driving?'

'Don't call me woman.'

'I didn't mean to insult you.'

There he was again. Joke or no joke. Insult or no insult. Hard to crack and tiresome with it. 'It's just . . . Justin called me that. It was an, an endearment, a compliment.'

Henry gave a snort of delight. 'I'm not surprised.'

Tears came easily to Bianca. Her emotions were near the surface, Justin had told her. It didn't in any way indicate weakness.

Nor did it this time, it gave her strength. 'I want to tell you why I broke my engagement with Andrew.'

'Why would that stop me driving?'

'Oh, do dry up about driving.'

'I loved Andrew very much. I know you don't believe me, none of you would except Rosa. It was because he was different, that was why, and of course his looking like that, and all he knew, and all he'd seen and all we would see together. Places I'd never heard of: Petra, Angkor Wat, Chichen Itza. I can remember them all, all the names and there were lots more. It was more than just his being an architect. He wanted to see the whole world, the wonders of it, to find out—and he wanted to show me. He seemed, I mean, to worship me—and don't look like that, I don't know how else to describe it.

'And all the other girls being besotted about him, I didn't

mind that either. Half the School of Architecture had crushes on him, boys and girls. That dark face, dramatic, always talking. None of us had ever seen anyone like him. All that, plus brains and brilliance. Remember?'

'Yes.'

'That was why I called him Andrew. Andy seemed—not large enough somehow. Not destined for the whole world. I know you hate it. I know you hate my talking about him at all but I'm going to. I'm going to go on and on and tell you everything, tell you why, and you can just keep driving like you said you wanted to and . . .'

He didn't look at her, he refused to look at her.

'Remember his clothes? Those beautiful shirts? Like Hamlet's, all wide sleeves and floppy collars. Andrew made his own patterns, everything. He made things for me and I wore them all, weird black things, all trailing. And shoes, you know he made himself a pair of shoes?'

'Yes.'

'Italian shoes he loved best of all. Women's shoes. He used to get his father to bring them back from Milan for me. Shoes like nothing in the world: four-inch heels, stilettos, stretch satins. And the colours: maple, tomato red, pistachio green, plum. They were works of art. Glorious things. I remember him picking up a pointy-toed one, you know how they were then, like a long black beak, and kissing it. Telling me what it would do for my legs. It is something to do with design, he said, the cutting. You land up slim as a model and six feet tall. They were magic, magic things. And Andrew, Andrew who loved me and wanted to marry me and be the best designer in the world, he knew all this. He knew it in Ponsonby in the '60s. You know what it was like then. You remember.'

'Yes.'

'He started borrowing the shoes, to show his design tutor, he said. Just one at a time. He kept them on the table by his bed so he could see them first thing, he said. He had several on the grotty mantelpiece. Then.'

She was weeping now, silently, the tears flowing down her face.

'One came back all stained. It was a red and blue leather peep-toe, real Rita Hayworth thing. He said he'd spilt coffee and he was sorry and I knew he was. It was ruined. He would write to the makers in Milan. They always have thirty-sevens. It is the classic size, he told me, and I felt quite proud. I know it's silly but . . .

'I had seen him that day already, he was doing honours then, and he came in to say hello and how about . . . I said no, I had to go into town to get my hair cut but I gave him some coffee and said I'd get home as soon as I could and when I got to Antonio's my man had been sacked, sacked that very day for putting his fingers in the till and they hadn't even told me. I thought, Blow this, I'm not having any old cutter, and Andrew will be waiting and Mum isn't home and I couldn't get there quickly enough.

'I'll never forget it. Never.'

'What?'

She was still weeping.

'I'm telling you. I'm telling you exactly. I knew he'd be in my bedroom with the shoes and I went in quietly to surprise him and tell him I loved him, and that Mum wouldn't be home for hours.

'I saw the curtain first, blowing out the open window and then his back view and his bare legs and I laughed and said something like he was a bit previous, wasn't he, and he swung round with a shoe, my pretty shoe in his hand and, he was . . .'

No.

'He was making himself come in my shoe.'

*

Henry pulled onto the verge and switched off the engine. Three black heifers ambled across the paddock to stare, spit swinging from their glum mouths, their tails moving slowly from side to side. The pine branches of the plantation tilted and swayed.

'Why are you telling me this?'

'I think you should know.'

'I did know,' he lied, slamming into gear. 'And I can't imagine what you're making all the fuss about.'

The car leapt forward, stones from the berm struck paintwork, the heifers turned tail to lumber across the paddock and stare again.

Henry did not know but he had guessed. Or perhaps suspected is a better word. Where there is brilliance, astonishment at life, there is often difference. It doesn't have to mean sad men flashing, it doesn't have to provoke sniggers, though it often does. The nudge, wink and nudge again formerly reserved for unlicensed pregnancies and homosexuality, the sneers and the leers of good keen men and women now include those who take their sexual pleasures differently and at one remove; the fetishists, the dresser-uppers, the transvestites, the 'kinky'. All of whose behaviour is perfectly legal. There are magazines now for those his father would have corralled into his catch-all word 'unwholesome'. Henry knew about paraphilia, had read about it after Andy killed himself, if he had. He knew the names for various forms of compulsive sexual behaviour, the terms for specific fetishes—rubber, fur, leather, dozens of them. That involving worship of female shoes is called retifism. Not an easy word to remember, retifism. It is found in men of every sexual orientation, the book had told him, but Henry knew that already.

If Andy were alive now he would be prancing off to the Shoeman's Ball, subscribing to *Fetish Times* or *Super Spikes*, surfing the internet for sources of information. Henry gave a long sniff. Andy should not have died.

He saw him fondling a lace-up stiletto, his palm sliding from the heel, up and over and down the toe, his face intent, his hand slow. 'Do you think I've got one of those weirdo things about shoes?'

Henry put *The Tin Drum* face down beside his infant son's blue knitted bear. 'I hope not.'

The smile was dreamy. 'I don't mind if I have . . . To me beautiful shoes are the perfect art form, the ultimate combination of design, engineering, colour. Look at this toe,' he said, stroking purple leather. 'And the heel—tomato, the bloom of tomato. No other word. It's the leather. You can't get colour and the *bloom* of colour in any other material. The depth.

'And Bianca realises all this, you know. Have you ever looked at her ankles?'

'Of course.'

'Her feet are even better. Narrow, wonderful shape. Beautiful feet are important to me. Very important. People with dirty feet, filthy cracked toenails, I find that . . .' Andy stood up, picked the blue bear from the sofa, punched its middle and dropped it. 'I find that repellent. Worse than repellent. I find it . . . immoral.'

Henry reached for the pipe he had smoked then. He lit up, relit, puffed hard, gave himself time.

'Do you love Bianca?'

'You nuts or something?'

'Not just her feet?'

Andy flopped down. The bear gave a small muffled squeak. 'I saw a film when I was a kid. About eleven or twelve. *Madonna of the Seven Moons*, it was called. The girl had gone mad or something and cleared out and the hero kept moping about looking for her. At one stage he said, "If I had ten dreams, Maddalena Labardi would be in every one of them."

I remember thinking, Shit.' He closed his eyes, opened them. 'You don't think I should hit you?'

'No.'

'Or that I'm a raving perve?'

'Get off that bloody bear.' Henry knocked it into shape, twitched its ears. 'No,' he said.

'Good,' said Andy.

He left soon after. Henry identified the body a week later.

'If you had loved him, really loved him, you would have helped him. Not dumped him, left him floundering—left him to . . .'

Bianca was now dry-eyed.

'I was twenty. My world was him and it had fallen apart. I was shaking, shaking like a leaf. I took all the shoes and threw them at him one after the other, on and on. I was screaming, out of my mind, screaming and screaming and then I ran.

'I never saw him again. You should be grateful to me. Be quiet, I haven't finished. Grateful. All that time, before the funeral, after, I never told a soul. I never said how I had loved him. Why I had stopped. Nothing.

'And I knew, the moment I saw him there, I knew. I knew he didn't love me, had never loved me. It was the shoes, those beautiful shoes. It was them he loved. I was just a thing, a thing for the shoes. I took them to the dump next day and I flung them, every one, further and further as far as I could and they looked terrible, I mean it, ghastly, like painted traps, something from another world, a jungle; brilliant petalled things that snap shut on insects and eat them alive. Digest them. All those heels sticking up and the colours, acid green and lime and purple and pink. There were mules, stilettos, sandals lying in all that rotten mess and the seagulls whirling and that smell, that sour, burning dump smell and I went home and lay in the bath for an hour and I knew I'd never get clean again.

'It wasn't me who killed Andrew. It was the shoes.

'I thought I would never get over it and I wouldn't have if it hadn't been for Justin. Not only losing Andrew. It was how. Why. And people, what they said. Had we had a row? Had he left a note? Your mother thinking it was my fault, blaming me for his death even after the coroner's verdict. I felt dirty, dirty beyond words. And I did for years.'

'You told *Justin*?'

'Of course I did and he saved me. He was a psychologist, wasn't he? He knew about obsessions, explained how it's compulsive, how they can't change. Andrew would never have loved me, he was incapable of loving, of being intimate, of caring. I was just an object, a thing with feet to dress up, to wear shoes.'

'Why did you ask me the other night if anything more had been discovered about Andy's death when you know every last detail, the tragic blinding waste of his death . . .' He paused for his answer, received none. 'And why are you telling me all this now?

'Why?' he said again.

Her voice was calm, her face serene. 'I think you owe me something, Henry.'

He laughed from release of tension, from the sheer bloody absurdity of the woman, from despair. Andy, Andy whom he had loved, the younger brother who outshone him and always had and so what, had killed himself. The brother he had minded for years, had bought condoms for, had talked things through with night after night. Andy had died alone and desperate. Not from genuine love of the woman beside him, he agreed with her there. But from the realisation that his obsession was untameable, that he had loved the wrong things and the wrong woman, he had drowned himself, had killed the whole to destroy the part. It was a long time ago.

Henry looked at the bridge foundation beside the motorway, the hexagonal blocks fitting together in neat concrete patchwork. He could swerve, accelerate, crash. And Bianca would survive and he would be crippled for life.

'What did you have in mind, Bianca?'

'I think,' she said calmly, 'you should buy that cottage in the paper this morning as an investment for Rufus. It's time Rufus settled down, got a proper job. And he and I could do it up and I could live in it. If it will suit my things, of course. I've never been really happy with the Bed and Breakfast idea. I don't think Justin would have liked that at all.

'It would be in my name and when I die I would leave it to Rufus. I am very fond of Rufus. I had planned to leave him something before all this awful muddle about my money and having to come out here and everything.'

Henry did look at her this time. His sick heart was thumping as he turned to her.

'And if I don't?'

'I will tell your mother why Andrew took his life.'

This laugh was louder. A victory roll, a sucks to you, a yah yah yah.

'She wouldn't believe a word of it, let alone understand. And if she did she'd kill you.' He thought of the still-bloodied tomahawk in Pukekohe, the stained block by the implement shed and laughed again.

'And what about Rufus?'

Henry was humming, bowling along the motorway on a sunny Saturday morning singing to himself: *We're three happy chappies with snappy serapes, you'll find us beneath our sombreros*. Where on earth had that come from.

'What about Rufus?' he laughed.

'Ros showed me all those shoes he sent her.'

An articulated truck thundered by, followed by a fire

engine screaming for room, room and more room.

'Three pairs,' said Henry. 'Only three.'

Bianca shook her head. 'Poor Ros,' she murmured.

He got home. He got them both home. He drove back to Meadowbank like an old man in pain, slowly and carefully. He drove in to the garage and walked up the path. Bianca collected her notes and followed him, her skirt brushing against some ragged pelargoniums which should have been trimmed back and of course hadn't.

five

Henry had not told Rosa. The words did not sound well. Your sister tells me, Rosalind, that my brother was a sexual pervert. She is about to hand on this intelligence to my mother unless I buy her a house. I see no reason why my mother should be troubled in this way so I have agreed to her suggestion.

Nor did disinterested generosity. I have decided, Rosalind, that I will buy a house for your sister. Rufus can help her do it up. It should be an excellent investment and we will get shot of her.

He saw Rosa, barefoot in an elongated T-shirt with kittens from Girlswear which served as a nightshirt. Why? When you said you wouldn't. How can we afford it?

We can't.

Then how?

I'll take out a new mortgage on this house.

At your age?

Silence was the other alternative. Until the morning, silence was best.

'Why can't I take her tea and toast as well?' he had asked weeks, months, years ago before Bianca arrived.

Rosa, naked except for a plastic shower cap, had patted

his buttock. 'Getting a bit saggy. Sort of pleated at the edges. Because eating in bed is sordid. Didn't you know?'

So there they were, due solely to Bianca's views on moral torpor, sitting up like vultures; munching, drinking, passing, nodding and passing again. Henry cleared his throat.

Rosa, caught in mid-dash to the kitchen, paused. Bianca lifted her head. Rufus continued rolling his own. He had smoked his last tailormade.

'I haven't had a chance to discuss this with you, Rosa,' said Henry, 'but I've decided we should all have a look at the cottage Bianca saw advertised yesterday.'

The reaction was gratifying. Like Mr Bennet's virgin daughters at their father's admission that he had called on the new neighbour, Rufus and Bianca were loud in their praise. Bianca clapped her hands, Rufus seized his father's. Only Rosa looked puzzled. 'Why didn't you tell me, Henry?'

'I meant to, but it slipped my mind.'

Rosa watched the interesting jiggle of light on the ceiling and traced it to her cup of coffee. Why, she asked, would light reflect back from her coffee?

No one answered.

'I'll take a picnic,' she said.

Bianca's pleasure heightened. She had wondered when the ham and egg pie in the fridge was going to appear. She enjoyed picnics and all small treats arranged by others and Rosa was good at arranging them, so things worked out well and always had. Bianca hoped Webster Street was not too far away.

It was near at hand, though not, unfortunately, within walking distance. The sign drooped from its post at the entrance to a previously unknown cul de sac. Old cottages had been pulled down and replaced by townhouses, the majority of which crouched low as they guarded their concrete sweeps, their lock-up garages, their hydrangeas and their tiny lawns. Others shot upwards, three storeys or more, all angles and unused balconies and pointed roofs.

'Postmodern crud,' said Rufus.

Henry, who was thinking of Andy's probable reaction, nodded.

'All the other old cottages have been gentrified,' continued Rufus. 'That's always a good sign.'

The land agent (call me Max) agreed.

'Why do they tart them up?' said Bianca. 'All that phoney ironwork.'

'That's not a problem with this one,' laughed Max. 'Mind you, you have to remember it's deceased estate.'

They saw what he meant, they saw immediately. Max was now talking rapidly. The beneficiaries of the estate would of course clean it out—all the junk would disappear. A lifetime of junk here, he said, kicking a mangle on the verandah as he shouldered his way beneath wisteria to unlock the front door. 'The mangle?' murmured Bianca. Yeah, the mangle would undoubtedly go. 'No,' said Bianca and Rufus simultaneously, 'We'll take it off their hands,' continued Rufus. 'Put it that way.'

The door swung open on to squalor and more finds. 'The butter maker also, if that'd be any help. Don't you agree, Bee?' Bianca nodded. 'If it's any help,' she agreed. 'In fact I'd go further. I would be prepared . . .'

She stopped. Rufus removed his foot from hers. They entered.

Bianca and Rufus moved around the house making small discreet mews of excitement at scrubbing boards, a copper, a wooden handle in the WC labelled *Pull*. Rosa and Henry stood close together, stupefied by the mess, the air of decay. The sense of human disintegration was overwhelming, palpable. There was plenty of evidence. Layers of newspapers lay on a table on which meals had been eaten and spilt. Someone had scrawled *Fuck off, Fraser* in large letters above the stained sink, empty beer bottles spilled from an unlocked shed.

It would be no problem at all for Rufus to get rid of that lot, he said, no problem at all.

The agent looked at him thoughtfully. 'That, of course, will have to be discussed with the vendors. Frankly, I was of the opinion that it should be cleaned out before we advertised. *Have your property looking its best at all times.* It's one of our best vendor tips. But of course you never know where you are with deceased estates.'

A floorboard creaked beneath his weight.

Rufus and Bianca were undeterred. Bianca began taking measurements with what Henry recognised with astonishment as his retractable tape from the garage, climbing nimble as a cat over discarded newspapers and last-gasp chairs to check and recheck and record the results in a small lined notebook.

Rufus was both professional and authoritative. Every aspect of the structural work was examined. He discovered bonuses; concrete piles, would you believe, and it was gibbed throughout except for the bedrooms. Otherwise not a scrap of scrim in sight. He was under the house for piles, up on the roof searching for leaks. Negative. He checked sash cords, knocked on walls. There was no insulation, he reported, but that was to be expected. Nothing wrong with the water pressure, the toilet was sound, the stove worked and the drains were as sweet as a nut.

Rosa wandered from room to room. It was a small house, two bedrooms, one recept, usual offices.

As Mother would have said, it sat out well to the sun. It would need to. Without sun the place would be insufferable. Rosa could see signs, glimmers of potential like those glimpsed in the faces of heroines in old movies before the hero takes off their glasses. The rooms were well proportioned, the ceilings high. Its bones were good, a help at any time but especially in decline.

She began to see Bianca and Rufus's point; enthusiasm, vision, is always infectious after the first shock.

She could see the three of them, Bianca, Rufus and herself, setting out each morning, hi-hoing their way off to their day's work. The clearing, the sorting and, above all, the discarding. Rosa enjoyed her visits to the tip, the dump, the landfill. She found them cathartic. Even the scrubbing, the refurbishing could be fun. Rufus would do the painting. Bianca would boss them rigid, Rosalind would bring the food. It would work out splendidly. She went to find Henry, who had disappeared. I have good vibes about this place, she would say.

But why had he changed his mind?

Henry was stumping about the tangled overgrowth of the ex garden, avoiding his wife. He had no wish to confide in her at the moment, or ever, but he would have to eventually. Reaction had set in. Why in God's name had he suggested this visit? He would have to consult Charlie Adamson about his finances. Everyone was so damn old. He needed, he thought with a stab of something like mirth, an entrepreneurial young man like Rufus. A spin doctor to transform a bad situation into good, to change his mindset. Which he could do himself, of course he could. Here he was, a man of plans, vision, an intelligent speculator, no, not speculator, a developer; a snapper-upper, a keen-eyed businessman.

He had assets, he had enough money, or could find it somehow. He saw his father, wealthier than he would ever be, his rampant moustache, his sad smile. 'I'm a terrible businessman, terrible.' A man with a talent for self-deception.

Henry turned to stride through knee-length grass. Positive, that was the thing to be. Positive. Rosa would not be impoverished, Bianca would be assisted and Rufus would be given a fresh start. And all because of his, Henry's, enterprise and initiative, his facing up to the situation, his turning bad news to good. He had put the right spin on Bianca's perfidy. He was doing something constructive. He would discuss things with his wife, he would explain everything. All would be well.

He tripped, tossed a dead bike wheel onto a mound nearby and trekked on to find the rest of the team.

Rufus was now on to rates, water rates, garbage collection, the proximity of schools. Max gave him his answers and told them other things. He told them the property was a patent to tranquillity. A handyman's special, like the ad said. Thirsty for a coat of paint inside and out, but think of the potential. He told them about location, location, location and to look at the lovely flow inside and out which was ideal for both formal or informal living. The place had one of the most conducive environments Max had seen in a long time.

'And what is the asking price?' asked Henry.

Max told him.

'Whaat!'

It was the location, Max explained. Location, location, location. He personally thought the vendors were perhaps a teeny bit unrealistic, still, early days, open to negotiation.

Henry opened his mouth.

'We'll let you know,' said Rufus quickly. 'Never hurts to make an offer, does it?'

'No.' Max laughed once more. 'Not if it's one we can pick up and run with.' And no, he didn't think the vendors would object to them having a picnic out the back.

Rosalind threw the bike wheel to one side and sat on the mound in her working shorts. Many of Rosa's belongings were categorised. She had walking shoes and sitting shoes, reading glasses and seeing glasses and an old pair for ironing.

She looked around at the collapsed tumble of the yellow

banksia rose plus clothesline. Buddleia had seeded itself. In summer, its lilac pendants would hum with bees. Rosa's eyes were bright beneath her pudding-basin haircut (Bianca), her change of heart evident. She took a large bite of ham and egg. 'Anything could happen here,' she said. 'Real *Secret Garden* stuff.'

'Oh, Ros,' said Bianca, 'you're so hopelessly romantic.'

Rosalind took another bite. 'Have you ever actually known anyone called Dickon?'

Silence.

'Even in books I've only known two. *The Secret Garden* and that Ngaio Marsh boiling-mud one. Such a good idea, the murderer changes the marker posts, remember? I always wondered whether she got it from *The Hound of the Baskervilles*, changing the markers, I mean. It's odd, isn't it, in the old ones, you don't mind how they die. Drowned in boiling mud! Imagine. And what was Dorothy Sayers' bell one?

'*The Nine Tailors*,' yawned Henry.

'Yes. Imagine being belled to death.' She looked around, loving them all, glad of plans, projects, people.

Henry leaned uncomfortably against a small lacebark.

Bianca was right. Rosa was a romantic. She had committed herself like a fool, had given her heart to the world, had made herself vulnerable to its pain and delights. Her attempts to give warmth to life impressed him, her determination to maintain affection in the endless muddle of the day by day left him speechless. He was grateful to Rosalind.

Bianca and Rufus sat side by side on a tarpaulin, their backs against a dilapidated crib wall, waves of empathy flowing between them. Rufus rolled a cigarette and offered it. 'Give it a go, Bee. You won't know till you try.'

Bianca took it smiling. She was happier than she had been for months, although it was a tiny bit disappointing that her slice of ham and egg pie had had no yolk. She liked yolk.

'It depends on the price, of course,' said Henry.

They left the wilderness to silence and the drone of two insistent bumble bees and drove home. Nobody spoke, there was no need to. The visit had been satisfactory, extremely so for some, and there was much to think about.

Trim houses flashed by, well-mown lawns were remown, a small child fell off a bicycle with trainer wheels and was brave. Meadowbank was at leisure on this warm Sunday afternoon, although nobody was to be seen demonstrating either rest or recreation. There were no bodies lying or even sitting outdoors. Leisure for Meadowbankers happened when they went somewhere else. When they arrived at a place labelled *Leisure* and knew they were there. A place where there was no grass to be shaved or cars to be cleaned and the shopping was out of this world.

Rosalind waved to Mr Desai on the corner, who lifted a small bunch of chrysanthemums in reply. He was handing over to his son, he had told her recently. Fifty years and not even Christmas Day off and now the supermarkets. There was no room left for the small man.

Rosa glimpsed the legs between Bianca and Henry's back views. Their owner stood on the top step beside the largest pack in the world.

'Gaby,' roared Rufus.

Rosa's arms opened in greeting but the young woman had been enfolded, engulfed, her legs were now glued against Rufus's, her face hidden by his embracing arms. Gaby stood tiptoe in Australian snakeboots; yards of black leggings were topped by a flared mini surmounted by a width of heavy beige lace. Over her black T-shirt she wore a brocade waistcoat in faded crimson and ivory stripes with rosebuds like the ottoman in Mother's bedroom. She slid a leg between Rufus's, raised her virtually shaved yellow-orange head to gasp for air and returned for more. She changed tack, was now sampling her man, making tentative little extensions of lips and tongue, coming at him from the side, above, below, like a male spider aware of the life-threatening aspects of courtship.

Rosa, Bianca and Henry stood staring; there seemed little point in doing anything else. This was a demonstration of affection.

Their reactions were different.

Rosa's hands were clasped in excitement, her mind already skidding through the contents of the deep freeze. Bianca's mouth was tight. This was not what she had in mind. Gaby's arrival was too sudden, too precipitate, *too like the lightning, which doth cease to be ere one can say it lightens.* And, what's more, Gaby would stay. And stay and stay. And she and Rufus had plans afoot, work to do together, like-minded comrades active in the cause. Damn. And blast.

Henry tugged his lip. Gaby was probably no worse than many of her predecessors in Rufus's affections, which had been wide-ranging and sometimes unusual and, furthermore, she had saved his son's life. But her timing was bad. Astonishingly bad, bad beyond bad peculiar. Bugger. Henry had planned to sit the team around the table and detail the conditions governing his suggestion. Special conditions would apply. Were Bianca and Rufus misguided enough to think otherwise? The question must be addressed without delay.

Gaby's bird-boned hand now lay in Henry's, her gaze from eyes the colour of peat tarns was unblinking, her hair yellow ochre stubble. She was astonishingly thin.

Rosa, wondering whether to welcome her with a kiss, decided against it. The narrow face seemed all red spectacle frames and angles and she was used to women who smiled.

'I hope you haven't been waiting long?'

'No sweat.'

And nor it was. If it had been, Gaby would have said so. Henry would bet money on that. Relax, Rosa, relax. We're dealing with nature here, untrammelled nature, forces of.

'I believe you saved Rufus's life,' he said loudly.

Gaby gave a wide grin, even the red frames brightened. 'Which time?'

'You remember, hon,' said Rufus quickly, 'getting me down from Poon Hill. Carrying the packs, all that?'

She shook her head, shared the joke with Henry. 'He colours the picture.'

Henry smiled back. He was not offended, anything but. He was pleased by this unexpected-looking young woman from Matamata where butterfat content is all, who had demonstrated within five minutes both passion for Rufus and acceptance of his endearing attributes. Henry had found a fellow researcher, a colleague. He felt like the animal behaviourist who put his eye to the keyhole and met that of the gorilla researching back. He had an ally in his field, a clear-sighted pragmatist, one who would be trusted not to massage the results.

'Yeah,' said Gaby now smiling proudly at Rufus, 'lies like a rug, don't you?'

Rufus demonstrated slicing his throat or hers.

Bianca smiled thinly.

Rosa was busy with the front door. 'Come in,' she said, 'come in.'

'Tell us about the wedding,' said Henry. 'Who was the bride?'

Gaby heaved her vast pack onto one shoulder. 'Gran. But he's a nice old guy. They did the hokey-cokey after they'd had a few beers.'

The hokey-cokey. Gran must be his vintage. The details of the dance were hazy. You put y'left foot in, y'put y'left foot out—then what? Perhaps Gran would teach him again one day. That would be nice.

And there was no reason why family discussions should not take place in front of Gaby, even if she had not saved his son's life in quite such dramatic circumstances as he had understood. Had coloured the picture.

Obviously Gaby, as a life-saving helpmeet and partner, had an interest in any family discussions.

'*Special conditions apply*,' said Henry, his eyes flicking around the table as he shuffled his notes.

Rosa was watching Gaby. Gaby, she decided, was her own person. 'Ashtray?' she murmured, lighting a cigarette. Bianca gave a small dry cough. Gaby offered her a cigarette, which was accepted. They shared the ashtray produced by Rosa. Bianca told Gaby that it was a present from herself to Rosa and she was glad to see it again. That it came from Andalusia. Gaby said, Was that right, and asked Henry why was it again they were here?

Gaby knew the essentials but she wanted details. Rufus had explained the situation to her after a quick connection in his bedroom, marred only by Rosa's arrival with sheets. Gaby had seized a towel and leapt to the knocked door. Why fuss. You're offered unwanted sheets by a small smiling grey-haired woman. You take sheets. You make up two beds, you sleep in one. You go with the flow, no problem.

She sat cross-legged on patchwork after Rufus's explanations and examined a verruca on the sole of her foot. 'Sounds okay.'

'And an old guy's going to leave a lot of money to Mum.'

'How much?'

Rufus didn't know. But still.

'Oh sure. Still.'

*

Gaby fixed her unblinking eyes on Henry's as he answered her query.

'Yeah, Roof told me that. But there's nothing to understand is there? I mean as regards "conditions". You buy the cottage after I've given it the okay.'

Bianca, caught on the back draught of shock and smoke, coughed. Rufus patted, Rosa ran. Water was provided. 'Why should you be consulted, Gabrielle?'

'Gaby. Because I'm his partner. He'd never dream of taking on anything without my okay, would you hon?'

Rufus nodded. 'Never have and never would.'

'Besides,' said Gaby, 'I'm a gun painter.'

Bianca was thinking. Another pair of hands would be useful, very useful. There was something Rufus had mentioned called sugar soap, which was required to bring up the old wood. She hadn't liked the sound of it. It could burn. You had to be careful, even with gloves. And all those high stud walls, who was going to get up there. Gaby. What a name.

'You might have told me of Gaby's talents, Rufus,' she murmured.

'You might have told us of Gaby.'

'Oh, give it a rest, Dad. I didn't know when she'd show up. We had a bit of an up and downer,' said Rufus, kneading the black-covered thigh beside him. 'Didn't we?'

'Yeah,' said Gaby vaguely. 'And the place will be in Roof's name?'

All hell let loose. Bianca and Rufus were shouting. Gaby the unknown sat silent, her head tipped to one side in attention.

Henry sat smiling in his chair with arms. He covered his mouth with his palm and winked at Rosalind. *Winked*. Rage and muddle and bad behaviour and all Henry could do was wink.

'Stop brawling,' she cried. They stopped, their faces quick

with surprise, Bianca's mottled, Rufus's a dull crimson. He took one of Gaby's cigarettes and offered it to Bianca. She took the peace offering without a glance and laid it in front of her unlit.

The scent of lemon blossom wafted through open windows; a fragrance flowing, stealing their senses all away, like it said in the carol. Rosa was about to remind them when Henry became operational.

'The first thing is the price,' said Henry. 'I will negotiate the price, I will consult Charlie Adamson, and take that look off your face, Rufus, get his advice as to the property's potential. If and when the price becomes more realistic, and I mean exactly that, I'll make an offer. The place is a wreck, it will take more than work, it will take money, and incidentally, Rufus, I'll want details of your and Gaby's competence and experience in this field.'

They were holding hands now, smiling those closed-lip smiles that indicate both intimacy and exclusion.

All the world loves a lover but not Henry. Or Bianca. Rosalind smiled at them, or as near to them as she could get. They were lovely. Quaint but lovely, and so young. Well, not Rufus perhaps. Thirty-five isn't as young as all that but Gaby looked like a punk eighteen-year-old. Not that she could be but her, how would you say, her wayward gaucheness made her seem even younger. She was vital yet impassive, as interesting as someone from another race or planet.

'Sure,' they said together, 'sure.'

'The next thing. The title will of course be in my name.' Henry lifted a hand. 'That is unappealable.' He felt faintly drunk. The freedom of power, the power of freedom, the desire of dominance, the dominance of desire. So many choices and all tasting good.

Gaby was not pleased. 'Unappealable?'

'Not open to appeal.'

Anger, and more than anger, and smouldering disgust from Bianca.

'Secondly, when the house can be lived in, the two of you,' Henry dipped his head to Gaby who stared back, 'three, will live there. Rent free for the moment but when it's liveable there will be a minimum rent to pay off the mortgage.'

Bianca snapped upright in her seat.

'Three, huh,' said Gaby.

'Sure,' cried Rufus. Very generous of you, Dad. Very generous indeed. I, we, that'd be great, wouldn't it, Gaby?'

Gaby was staring thoughtfully at Bianca, who stared back. Cold peat met blue ice, neither faltered. Bianca lifted her unlit cigarette, lit it with Rufus's lighter and smiled at the younger woman. It was in now, that blank, sexless look, but it wouldn't last. And Rufus was devoted to his Aunt Bee.

Gaby lifted one shoulder and dropped it. 'Hard to know,' she said.

Bianca smiled.

'One final thing, Rufus, which concerns you only.'

Rufus turned to him, happy with plans and enthusiasm. 'Yes, Dad?' The little suitcase days surfaced, Henry's elation dissolved.

Who's kidding whom, you clown. You're not helping your son from disinterested affection. You've been blackmailed into it by that woman, that woman preening herself across the table. Bianca's presence was beginning to make him feel physically sick.

Cowardice in fellow crew members, he had read in some Battle of Britain memoir, had not been treated with the contempt reserved for braggarts. Unlike bull artists, cowards were felt to have some unfortunate deficiency for which they could only be pitied, such as colour blindness or poor vision.

Not a helpful memory. Why had he allowed himself to

slip into Bianca's trap like a rat to its drain? Rufus's sexual preferences, he was sure, did not stray from irredeemable heterosexuality. Mrs Felton would laugh at Bianca's disclosures about Andy and reach for her tomahawk.

Henry looked at his wife. Her attention had strayed. She would be thinking about five down or four across or wondering whether the labelless carton in the deep freeze was plums or boeuf bourguignon and if so would it do five.

He heard Bianca's murmur on the motorway, saw the calm hands, the crocodile tears. 'Poor Rosa.'

My sweet Rose, my dear Rose, be merry.

And she would. Henry would see to that. He must.

He thinks I don't know, but I do. I don't know what is going on because he hasn't told me, which I find odd. But I do know that something is, and furthermore I don't like it. The atmosphere in this house is troubled, muddy, up the wop and out of kilter. There is an air of tension in both the formal and informal living areas, the flow is disturbed. I don't like it.

Why is Henry so troubled? Why is Bianca as smug as a cream-ingested marmalade cat? I can see why Rufus is happy, bless his heart, and I am sure Gaby will grow on me. I smile at Gaby. Again.

Gaby removed her over-sized red plastic spectacles, blew on them, rubbed them clear and replaced them. They were very large and glasses are small now. But Gaby, as Rosalind already knows, is her own person. She likes big ones. You get big ones. Yeah.

Rosalind's brief glimpse of the unshielded tawny eyes was startling. Gaby's eyes are weak, unfocused. She cannot see well. There is a chink in her armour. Goodness me and fancy that.

'As I was saying,' said Henry. 'This condition concerns you alone, Rufus.'

'Yes, Dad, you said.'

'I have decided to offer you a position in Felton Fabric Importers.'

Rufus ducked his head, stared from beneath his brows like shy Di from childcare days, when it was all good, when the romance had lifted the hearts of millions.

'Bit sudden, isn't it?' he said. 'You know me, Dad, I'm not much of a nine-to-five man. And besides, how would I get on to fixing up Webster Street? There's a ton of work to be done there. You said so yourself. It'll take months.'

'Webster Street,' said Henry, 'is not in the bag. Webster Street depends on my being able to make suitable financial arrangements. Do you,' he snapped, 'want your mother to be flung out of this house into the . . . into the street,' he said, resisting 'gutter' at the last moment, 'because it has been mortgaged for you and your friends?'

'What do you think I am?' Rufus hugged Rosalind, smiled at Gaby. 'We are.' He leaned forward to place his cards on the table. 'But how will you finance it otherwise?'

'I'll go and see Charlie Adamson.'

'Good thinking,' said Rufus.

'This is not a sudden decision. I've been thinking about it for some time. It is now or never, Rufus. A keen young thruster at forty is no longer young or a thruster. There's room for one more now Martin's gone. I had hoped to get by, it's a fine balance. And if I do give you a chance, take you on, train you, it's on this condition only: that the importing of textiles is your profession—other activities, if you insist on pursuing any, will be expendable as side salads. Is that quite clear?'

Gaby was all eyes. All eyes and bones and frames. She grabbed her lover's arm. 'Hey, Roof . . .'

Rufus ignored her. 'Well, Dad, my plans, our plans I should say, are a bit fluid at the moment.' He paused, thought, paused again. 'But I'd like to find out how things operate. Very much. Very much indeed.'

'And one other thing. It will involve you coming on a buying trip with me to Milan. Quite soon. Milan's the nub of things for us. We've been there far longer than anyone else here, got the contacts . . .'

Rosalind was staring at him. Why on earth hadn't he told her? We should have discussed it, talked things through. What is he *doing*, this man?

'Thanks to Martin,' she snapped.

Henry glanced at her in surprise, flung her a crumb and returned to Rufus. 'To Martin, as you say, but not entirely. It's essential that you come with me to get a glimpse of the way things work, meet the people, shake the hand. These things are important in Italy.'

'As they are anywhere,' murmured Bianca, 'Justin used to say . . .'

With vicious stabs Gaby ground her cigarette butt onto glazed blue pomegranates. She had no wish to return to Milan, not at the moment. Rufus could get her boots. But to be left with this lot . . . She chewed her lip, thought hard. Milan? Meadowbank? Meadowbank? Milan?

'I'll stay and get cracking here,' she said.

Henry, hiding his amazement, agreed that would be a good idea. How had she thought, envisaged for a micro-second that she would do otherwise.

He turned with relief to Rufus.

Who was concentrating. Henry could hear his mind ticking. His hands were clasped tight in the same excited gesture which had greeted his first bottle of ink. He had walked up Queen Street to the car park, clutching his treasure in its little saw-edged paper bag, his face wearing the beatific smile of an acolyte with a chalice. That is one of the things about an only child, there is no confusion of childhood memories. There is only one fount. He smiled at his son.

'It will mean you starting on Monday week. Depending, of course, on what Charlie Adamson thinks. And if my offer is accepted.'

'And what is your offer?' asked Rufus.

Henry told them.

'You're joking.'

Bianca was not concerned. She knew the cottage would be purchased. There might be a bit of confusion until she had sorted out the title, but never mind. Never mind at all. Speed bonnie boat. All will be well and all manner of things will be well. Except . . . 'But you said, Henry, that Rufus would help do it up.'

'And so he will. In the weekends.'

'The *weekends*.'

'And statutory holidays. Also, there is an enormous amount of culling out required. You and Gaby can do that before the real work begins.'

Gaby and Bianca eyed each other. Gaby lit another cigarette, dragged deeply, exhaled smoke with the assistance of her protruding bottom lip.

'And me,' said Rosalind. 'I like taking stuff to the dump.'

Bianca's eyes caught Henry's. He looked away.

Charlie Adamson thought it was an excellent idea. A snip at that price but would they get it? They did. Rufus and Bianca were euphoric. They shared a love of both bargains and projects. They had vision. The cottage and the job offer had come at a good time. Rufus was aware of the need to consolidate his commercial expertise. As he told Gaby while they explored each other in his bedroom beneath the unseeing gaze of Auckland Grammar School classmates, a stint in a well-established business never did anyone's CV any harm. Especially when the firm belonged to his father.

He was glad he'd had the sense to inscribe the names on the back of the seventh-form photo. You never know your luck with school contacts.

Gaby remained thoughtful.

six

Rufus tried. 'But that's what business class is all about, Dad. You arrive rested, full of attack and ready to roll.'

They travelled as Henry had always travelled, strapped in knee-jerking economy, his shoulder propping the heads of strangers, his stomach belching in another's dreams. Occasionally father and son lifted a glass to each other as they discussed their plans, ran through their programmes. It was a productive flight. Henry enjoyed his son's company, marvelled at his instant rapport, his interest in each and every fellow traveller he was lucky enough to meet.

The American overlaying him on the other side confided that he had a weight problem. Rufus commiserated, his bright head nodding in sympathy. The man rubbed large pale hands on tightly encased thighs and moved on to jet lag. Did Rufus suffer from jet lag? No? Had he any idea how lucky he was to be spared? Jet lag had made serious inroads on the man's stability, had jeopardised his career expectations. The only thing was vitamins. Vitamins helped. He offered vitamins. Rufus took two rust-coloured tablets.

The man looked at him thoughtfully. 'Only thing, they make you randy as a goat, a goddamn hairy goat.'

Rufus's concern did not falter. He was a good listener.

Henry, who had been wondering why a hairy one, weren't they all, had forgotten that. You don't meet many good listeners, not people who take a genuine interest in another's problems rather than just sign off and wait for them to stop bleating.

Rufus had learned quickly in his four weeks at the firm, had been happy to start at the bottom, to understand every aspect; it was the only way to suss the whole thing out, in his opinion. He knew the names of the staff members in a day, which was not the achievement it would have been in his grandfather's time. He had been pleasant to Lorraine, had commiserated with her over her outdated software and been rewarded by smiles. He had liked the two men. Good guys. Didn't Dad think a few bonding sessions, the whole team nutting things out together would be a good thing? No, said Henry. The whole team comprised five people; Gary and Tim knew the job backwards, as did Lorraine.

But why had the staff shrunk like this? Rufus remembered when he was a kid. There had been double this number, the typists had given him sweets. Tessa.

Henry explained carefully. Things had changed in the textile business and would change further. Many textile manufacturers now have their own agents in Italy and have begun to have them here. Technology, global technology, entrepreneurial skills—all that is your field. Why I have offered you the job. The small man, said Henry, is struggling. Ask Mr Desai.

Then we change with them. Give people what they want. Cheaper range.

I sell quality merchandise.

They left it there for the moment. Henry reminded himself that he would not change, that the firm needed to, and that Rufus, as well as being quick on his feet and having his finger on the pulse, showed both aptitude and enthusiasm for the work. He was lucky to have him.

He wondered why he had not insisted on this career move for his son long ago, but knew the answer. Twenty years ago parental interference in one's children's choice of career had died, had crawled away to the Valley of the Bones to lie beside arranged marriages and pork pie hats and centre partings.

Your offspring's lives are their own, their choice must be untrammelled, they must lead their own lives. All sentiments with which Henry agreed wholeheartedly.

But nothing is simple. A neighbour had found his fourteen-year-old daughter climbing back into her bedroom from a school dance in the '60s. She confessed with shame that she hated it, all of it, all, had wanted to come home from the first minute but didn't want to admit failure. Oh Mum, oh Dad. Do I have to?

Or take born-again Christians. God will lead his children to the way, the lifestyles, the careers. But what if God doesn't. Lets his guidance slip, wants his children to be happy like any other loving parent. What if he withdraws into his all-embracing wisdom and lets them get on with it. Offers them freedom to make their own mistakes and go to hell in their individual handcarts. Decisions, decisions, decisions.

Henry was grateful for his second chance. Such thoughts, such self-engendered convolutions of the mind had, he felt sure, never occurred to his own father, that foolish, autocratic old man. Mr Felton had founded the firm, been successful and handed it on to Henry. That was what fathers did and elder sons accepted. There had been no discussion, no demur. Mr Felton would have been happy 'to make room for Andy', if it had been necessary, but was relieved when his younger son showed no interest. He was brilliant, Andy, undoubtedly brilliant, but was he perhaps too *sudden*, too, how could he put it, too mercurial for the day-to-day work of running a business; for the buying and the selling, the cut and thrust with textile manufacturers whose forebears' spinners and weavers had operated in Italy for five hundred years. In an uncharacteristic burst of metaphor Mr Felton had enlarged upon this to Henry. Andrew was excellent quality, first rate, but not made for hard wear; shimmering luminous stuff made for high days and holidays, not the plain slog of every day.

Henry, he told him, was also good quality, top grade. He would wear forever. An honest worsted, a bird's-eye perhaps. Henry need not fear. He too had style.

'Thank you,' said Henry.

It was impossible to tell how much the old man's attitude to life had to do with his younger son's death, but had he known the truth he would undoubtedly have been as appalled as Bianca. No cross-weave, no grey tones, had ever blurred the black and white patterns of his father's thinking. He was right, always and in every detail, and insisted on being recognised as being so.

'It was Wednesday not Thursday,' he shouted, apropos of something completely unmemorable—the day of the last bus strike, the loss of the cufflink, that extraordinary leader in the *Herald*.

'Thursday,' said Andy happily munching corned beef.

'I said Wednesday!'

'Yes, and I said Thursday.'

'Wednesday!'

'Okay,' said Andy cheerfully. 'Make it Wednesday.'

'But you don't believe me,' cried his father.

'No.'

'But I'm right.'

'Okay. You're right.'

'But . . .'

Andy forgave him. He reached across, patted the wrinkled skin of the hand beside him. 'You're not alone, Dad. Thousands of people would rather be right than happy.

Wednesday it is.'

Andy was quick and ruthless in his placement but knew when to stop.

Would he have killed himself if his father had been less terrified of difference and appalled by change?

Mr Felton had died soon after his favourite son, broken-hearted by his unnecessary death, which he hugged to his heart as one more piece of incontrovertible evidence that the world was going to the dogs. Brilliant young men had not slipped and drowned while fishing in his day.

His very stupidity was heartbreaking.

His wife had been glad to move out of Meadowbank when he died. She had kept her own counsel and continued to do so at Pukekohe. She was a strong woman, Mrs Felton.

It occurred to Henry that Rufus's career move, this promising surge of intelligent interest and enthusiasm for the world of fine fabrics, was directly attributable to Bianca's devious manipulations. He dismissed the thought, glanced with affection at his son chewing aphrodisiac vitamins beside him.

The man with the weight problem leaned across Rufus, his large pallid hand offering Henry succour from jet lag. Henry declined. He did not wish to feel amorous in Milan.

He sighed and fastened his seatbelt. He would ring Rosa tonight. Rosa, he would say, be happy, Rosa. Rufus is a fine young man but we have always known that, have we not. His eyes, for some unknown reason, filled with tears; not tears, just excess. Rosa had never been to Milan.

'I'd much rather take you when I retire,' he had explained. 'Then we can have fun together and I'll show you everything and you'll have one of those books labelled *My Trip* and we'll have thousands of photographs and bore people rigid.'

*

'Where are you going?' said Henry. 'The bus is this way.'

Rufus put his hand luggage down and shook his curls. '*Cherubino*,' giggled a young woman with *Imagination on Tour* plastered across her front. Where had it gone, Henry wondered, this instrument of creation which had left home.

Flushed, distracted by bosoms, irritated by the petty meannesses of age, Rufus had had enough.

'For God's sake, Dad, let's get a taxi. I'll pay.'

'Good,' said Henry and whose money was it anyway and yes, why not.

It was Sunday, he had forgotten that. *Domenica* would be in red on the calendars. In summer, families would be at leisure in the open spaces they passed. Spaces which then would look like flowering paddocks. Or meadows; paddocks don't flower. Italians seem able to accept the fact that grass grows and is green and does not have to be eaten or shaved to extinction; that daisies and buttercups may flower and children may roll and picnics may happen beside crumbling stone.

But not today. The spring air was cold. Softball was in progress but few spectators huddled beneath the gnarled stumps of the plane trees, one or two of which had begun to shoot. Perhaps resurrection, life itself, would make more sense in a land of deciduous trees.

In a drear-nighted December,
Too happy, happy tree,
Thy branches ne'er remember
Their green felicity.

Anthropomorphic rubbish and maudlin to boot.

Henry watched the dark cypresses swaying. In Meadowbank a neighbour amputated their heads with a chainsaw. He liked them neat.

Twice a year, autumn and spring, autumn and spring forever, he had travelled this straight road, had noted the window detail, the pediments, the small balconies which seemed designed for papal blessings, the ancient buildings which fade from terracotta to rose as the sun goes down.

He liked it here, love and the past returned each time he came, came with the first spring catkins against stone, the first stench of diesel, the white magnolia buds clinging to bare branches like small sleeping cockatoos. He liked old buildings and the fragrance of orange trees.

Hotel Garibaldi was a small old-fashioned hotel with a tiny hesitant lift, a place of dark wood and small lobbies on each floor furnished with a solitary chair and nothing more. All the rooms, or any Henry had met, were small. Every one had a large, dark wardrobe, an even larger window with a venetian blind and little else. At some stage during the last ten years formica-topped refrigerators had appeared in each room, and the full restaurant service had departed. Breakfast only was served in a room beside the magnolia tree. But the hotel was clean, there were business facilities available and it was situated in the heart of the fashion centre, the golden triangle of designer fashion; shops, boutiques and designer offices lay on every side. Location, location, location.

And the staff were pleasant. There is something endearing about a symbiotic relationship between hotelier and guest which is renewed twice a year for years with the same manly embrace beneath the vast ziggurat light-fitting in the low-ceilinged lobby. And Signor Battista spoke English.

And had known Carla. Had understood.

Henry introduced Rufus. Signor Battista was delighted.

'You are a lucky man,' he told Henry and pumped his hand once more. 'Congratulations.'

'Excuse me,' said Rufus, 'I'll just go and have another look at the lions.'

'Ah,' said Signor Battista, 'they all love the lions.'

*

I can't think why I did that. I'm thirty-five for Christ's sake, but I still want to have a good look. To see them immediately once we've got shot of the luggage and Dad'll be under-tipping some poor guy and I'd rather be out of it anyway.

It's raining now. And cold. The stone walls of the hotel are slick as silk. The two stone lions, or rather heads of lions, stand shoulder high on either side of the entrance door which swings and hisses as people come and go shaking umbrellas.

The lions stare back at me, their foreheads furrowed above retracted snarling jaws and stone fangs. Their manes are full, deeply carved and flattened at the back.

I can see why men like Heseltine are described as leonine. Tough, really. These are humanised lions, haughty old men lions, lions usurped but defiant. They remind me of Dad. Two Dads. The same hair, the same lift of the head so that, if you're not careful, you're looking up damp nostrils. The same hauteur.

Not that I've thought of Dad as up himself before. I have thought of Dad as a guy who is around. A cool old guy. I've seen him wear a cravat and still look human. A man with style.

You'd know if you have it and I've never given a stuff, who does. But the Italians on the plane, the guys in the hotel, you notice their clothes.

We've had rows about it in the past. Not rows, it's difficult to have a row with Dad. Discussions maybe.

You've got it all wrong, Dad, I'd say. Then him looking at me, pretending he's exhausted, surprised. Whatever. Stirring me up with courtesy. Keeping his cool.

In what way, Rufus?

You get your suits made . . .

I'm a fabric importer.

. . . by a bespoke tailor.

All tailors are bespoke. It means made to order.

At great expense.

Most works of art are expensive.

Why bother?

Because they look better. They feel better. If you had a well-cut suit, Rufus, your bum wouldn't stick out.

He's a specialist in the dirty crack, the sort that goes off in your head and you're meant to laugh.

I just can't see the point of paying for bespoke . . .

You don't have to spit. It's a perfectly normal word.

. . . suits, yet you keep driving an old heap and putting up with that crap in your office at home.

You're confusing money with style, with having an eye, with meaning to dress as you do. Gaby has it. Your Uncle Andy had it . . . It's something given. And it lasts.

'His didn't,' I remember saying.

I thought for a moment he was going to hit me. But as usual he just oiled out of it. 'No,' he said. 'It didn't.'

'When we buried Andy,' he said suddenly, 'I insisted he wore his pink leather tie and a yellow silk handkerchief in his pocket.'

I laughed. I couldn't help it. 'What did he look like?'

He looks at me, his eyes cold as marbles in frost. 'Different,' he says.

Henry sat beside his son stirring coffee. His jet lag seemed to be getting worse. No sleep last night, no sleep for a week last time when he arrived home. Age, he supposed, or lack of vitamins, but a bugger either way. He finished his coffee, thought of the randy fat man without sympathy. Did he have work to do, people to see, experts to meet on their own ground, snap decisions to make amid the bustle and roar of machinery. Not many manufacturers could afford the luxury of the offices in Milan they planned to visit today, discreet, well-hidden marble spaces within walking distance of the Garibaldi.

The designers' garments displayed in the small windows on the Via della Spiga were visible to all. Tourists crowded the narrow streets, staring at suede shirts with the sheen and colours of silk—coffee, ivory, coral. Two old women stood lost in awe before a window of brightly lit glass pillars. On the highest, enshrined, lit from below, above and all around, sat a single silver kid sandal with a five-inch heel. There was no price tag.

Skirts were still short but they could only hope for better things when they saw the new season's range at the factories. It was high time skirts came down. Ridiculous and bad for trade.

Henry stopped before an androgynous-looking white polystyrene model in the window. It wore a panama hat dipped low over vacant eyes above a bright pink jacket. A yellow silk handkerchief flopped from the breast pocket of the jacket.

He walked on in silence, his heart racing.

'Hey,' said Rufus.

'Yes,' he snapped. 'I saw it. Come on.'

Monte Napoleone was full of small, busy-fingered women calculating in yen. Never in their wildest dreams had they expected such prices. The skirt. How much was the skirt? Calculator buttons buzzed in astonishment. Giggling women demonstrated collapse on crowded pavements.

They liked the shoe shops best, as had Rufus and Gaby. They had looked last time, she had tried on dozens of boots. But they were on their beam ends, not a show of buying. She had shoplifted a long-handled shoehorn by mistake, she discovered later. He had told his father about it. Not the shoehorn, why bother, but the hours they'd spent while she'd tried things on. How much he'd enjoyed it, just watching. How he must get her a pair, two pairs, they'd be half the price here.

'I wouldn't bet on it,' said Henry. 'Some of these characters' wares are so expensive they're not even imported at home.'

'How do you know?'

'I've been coming here a long time.'

Since before you were born.

An image flicked into his mind. Rufus aged about fifteen, red-faced and breathless on his bed, clutching a towel. 'Why the hell didn't you knock?' Henry closed the door. 'Sorry, it didn't occur to me.'

He sat on the end of the bed and glanced around, then smiled at his son. 'Your hair'll drop out,' he said.

He would never tell Rufus about Andy. It was pointless and besides, he was the one who wanted Andy to rot in peace did he not.

Let him lie. Any young death is tragic. *Whom the gods love die young* is a lie perpetuated by ancients.

Perhaps it was his vitamin-deficient jet lag or the emotional shreds of loss that brushed against him at unexpected moments in this city which had temporarily made him forget his love for it. There were too many memories, too many glimpses to remind. Things sneaked up on him, even now. The droop of a dark female head, a play of light, an unexpected reflection.

These small shocks did not occur at home, these disconcertings which made him think death might not be such a bad idea. That there was a lot to be said for a sleep and a forgetting. For being tucked up in a nice padded bespoke box and laid to eternal rest. Or not. Same difference, as Rufus would say.

He tried self-discipline. Not his strong suit. Carla has been dead for six years. You lost her ten years before. Stop this maudlin wallowing.

He smiled to himself, distracted by a sugar-plum fairy outfit in an adjacent window.

A grey-haired vendeuse reaching into the window for a pair of pink frosted-almond shoes smiled into his eyes, lifted the shoes in greeting and backed out. How do Italian women know that they are not only beautiful and desirable but will remain so? If they play their cards right, if they pay attention to their appearance and, preferably, marry rich men.

But it is more than that. They must have learned the habit of sensual pride at an early age. Like a love for your native landscape, it must be as familiar as the air you breathe for conviction to take hold, let alone stay with you forever. Some people, would you believe, find the Desert Road boring.

'The major problems in this business,' said Henry in the cab on the way out to Cernusco, 'are time and money. How much can you spare of each? There's never enough time, three days maximum . . .'

'It used to be longer than that when I was a kid.'

'Longer?' Henry's smile hung in the air. 'Well, things were more relaxed in those days.'

'I remember clearly. Eight sleeps at the beginning then count down every night till, boom—there you were.'

'So I was. With presents.'

'Yeah.'

The present buying had bored Carla. Bored her rigid. She had trailed behind him, chosen impossibly expensive gifts for his wife and child and laughed at his parsimony when he replaced them on their shelves. He told her not to come, he told her she was being ridiculous. She agreed and stalked off weeping. The pattern was repeated every time.

Every emotionally loaded gift was received with pleasure in Meadowbank and sat around for years, disturbing his peace of mind. As it should, should it not? As it did; Italian fire engines, handguns, bears. Why had he *let* her come? Why had he not sneaked out, snatched, grabbed, hidden the evidence? Thought of a better way. Stop thinking, man, stop thinking.

'You're sure you can cope on your own at Prato tomorrow?' he said.

'Of course.'

'I could come, there are things here to tidy up but, as I say . . .'

'Dad, for Christ's sake . . .'

'The first problem then. Money. How much can you afford to spend? Now this sounds easy at this remove. We've got it all worked out for Prato, as we have for Como today. You've got all the details, how much viscose, how much lycra, how much money we can spare. But it's not so easy on the spot. You'll see today.' He paused. 'You realise they've been making fabrics at Prato for five hundred years.'

'You said.'

'*The Merchant of Prato*.'

'I know.'

'Have you read it yet?'

'Dad,' sighed Rufus, 'I'm not fussed about some old guy's business five hundred years ago.'

Suddenly, unexpectedly, he remembered the lions' heads. They looked tired. Arrogant but tired, hanging on in there against the odds. His father was going to have to be informed, dragged into the real world. 'The future of the fabric industry,' said Rufus, 'lies in man-made fibres.'

Henry glanced up in surprise, not so much at the words but at the pomposity of his tone. Rufus was making a statement, issuing an edict. His grandmother was to suck eggs and would be shown how. Amusement kept Henry calm. The pontiff's bull had gone off at half cock.

'They have their place, certainly,' he said, 'and in this, as in every other fabric, except possibly the fine woollens of France, Italy leads the world. It's just a fact of life. Their designs, their textures, colours, fashion sense, the way the fabrics fall, their feel. I have never known an Italian manufacturer or designer without this feel, this literal and physical feel for quality, man-made or otherwise. Their viscose acetates, for example, are top of the range, and expensive.'

'Big money,' said Rufus.

'I thought you liked big money.' Henry was angry now. Bored by his beautiful switched-on son who was exactly what Felton Fabrics needed did it not.

He changed the subject. 'And remember, they're not so concerned about their image in Prato as they are up here. Tuscans are different. Don't go down tomorrow expecting to see the grandeur of the places we'll see today. These Como families have been the most famous silkmakers in the world since the eighteenth century. Made the best quality linens. They're not interested in man-made fabrics. These are proud men. Serious silk. Serious linen. Serious men.'

Rufus said nothing. Thank God he was going to Prato alone. He couldn't see the point of coming to Como at all. Prato had more reasonable linens, cheaper wools and an infinitely better man-made range. Okay, it had been producing fabrics, leading the world for five hundred years, but it was still funky, upfront, fun. Someone in Prato, he had heard, was into designer PVC. He had seen a woman in the street yesterday in a white PVC jumpsuit with a silver plastic handbag formal and unyielding as the Queen's. Drop dead glamour. Tomorrow today. Italian silks, in Rufus's opinion, were a dead duck.

China, Japan, the whole of Asia was where that market lay. He glanced at the old Europhile beside him with something like compassion. Henry had never quite got it together somehow. Had always been behind the eight ball. He couldn't wait to get Gaby into the firm. They would take off like a rocket, two rockets.

The back of her neck came to mind, the perfection of her sculptured ear, her narrow wrist. He closed his eyes. Gaby.

The reception area of Casa Monti was both grand and understated. Grey marble floors, green marble pillars, good lighting and one serene woman seated behind what looked like a slab of onyx. The only piece of technical equipment in sight was a reproduction antique brass telephone alongside a large round bowl containing two goldfish.

A mistake, thought Rufus. Over the top. Blown it. One or the other but not both.

The fronds of a huge palm tree almost brushed the woman's shining blue-black hair. She did not duck. She knew, perhaps, that tension is created by small gaps.

She smiled at them, glanced at Rufus and smiled again. He was becoming used to both the look and the smile. A smile and a look, he assumed, not unlike that which Gaby told him she received from her grandmother every time she went home to Matamata. A quick glancing sweep upwards. Friendly but enquiring, not quite sure. Pregnant or not? Slobbish or quaint? It was a look which made Rufus feel, not unsure of himself, no one can do that unless you let them, but an object of unwanted interest. He concentrated on the fish.

Which were behaving oddly. Very oddly indeed. One languid goldfish drifted, an ox-blood one flashed past at speed followed by another slow drifter through weed. Another flash, and an electric blue shot by. Rufus turned to the floor-to-ceiling windows on to the street in search of answers. Of course. The upside-down reflections of cars were reduced to fish size and encapsulated in the bowl. It seemed a pity the fish didn't know. He must tell Henry.

Henry was explaining that they had an appointment. The receptionist's smile agreed. How could they possibly have stumbled into this palace without one. She stroked the antique telephone into action, spoke and nodded. Her gentle replacement of the receiver, her smile, indicated the smallest delay in the world.

'Signor Monti sends his apologies, gentlemen. He will be with you in seconds. He is with the button lady.'

In fact he was with them in minutes. Minutes in which Henry had time to explain that this was by no means and must not in any way be interpreted by Rufus as power games, delaying tactics or a put down. This was a compliment, an acknowledgement that Henry was of the *cognoscenti*. Henry would know the importance of the button lady, he would probably know her name (which he didn't), he would undoubtedly know the name of the firm she represented (which he discovered later he did). The best firm in Italy, the most esteemed makers of the best buttons in the world and God lurks in the detail, does he not. Signor Monti's designers were begging for answers. The final decision from the top could not wait a moment longer.

Signor Monti came through a heavy glass door. Tall, large, with a profile from a Roman coin, he came to greet his friend, to welcome his friend's son.

The welcome was genuine, completely genuine, and pretty to watch. Signor Monti and Henry embraced with enthusiasm, the sheer pleasure at meeting again engulfed the two old men.

The last time Rufus had seen anything approaching such warmth had been between two black men farewelling each other in Tottenham Court Road; their ritual leave-taking had been as stylised as the mating dance of some exotic bird. They shook hands and swung away, spun back on their heels to clasp each other's wrists, separated for a high five, gave one final prolonged and laughing shake of the hands and, with springing feet and heads held high, went on their way rejoicing.

'Come,' said Monti, 'come to my showroom.' The pride of the man made his jowls shine, his gestures widen. He had something to be proud about; the age and history of the family company, its impeccable reputation, all pleased him. The grandeur of the building, the quality of the product spoke both for him and his deceased forebears. His pride, Henry knew, would not allow him to discuss his own son's views in front of Rufus. His son wanted change. Signor Monti knew the fabric industry was changing. There were newcomers even in Como. *Arrivistes* messing about in studios. Men and women described by his son with approbation as wacky. What is this wacky, he had asked Henry last time they met.

They had moved on to the changing dress habits of the wealthy young, their anything goes, their lack of respect for family traditions. Romeo did not want to go into the family business, could Signor Felton believe that. Signor Felton could and did. All that had surprised him had been Signor Monti's surprise.

He saw the old man looking sadly at Rufus. Rufus was at his best, attentive and serious and anxious to learn. It was a pity about his suit, but Rome, after all, was not built in a day. Henry was tempted to come clean, to relieve the old man's wistful envy with facts. My son, Signor Monti, wishes to diversify, which is his euphemism for lowering the quality of merchandise stocked by Felton Fabrics. I fear that, as far Rufus is concerned, for Como and, in particular, the top of the range fabrics manufactured by you, Mr Monti, it's Goodnight, nurse. Can you believe that, you good old man.

The showroom was an extension of the factory, a large space humming with noise and activity. The owner of the company was both its life blood and its soul. Employees dashed up to consult, waved bits of fabric in his face, were answered with voluble despatch; men and women stood back as they passed. Signor Monti's voice lifted, he called for *pezzo*, *pezze*, more, more, like a director shouting for light on an already well-lit stage. Workers moved to tug out rolls and more rolls. Signor Monti touched, stroked, sighed with pleasure and begged Henry and Rufus to do the same.

He became more excited, his gestures more dramatic. He rubbed a brocade, stroked a silk velvet, held a patterned silk of green, bronze and apricot to his ear as though listening.

The decisions, the thinking on the feet began. The company had not entirely finished their sample collections, no one had yet, but the ones here were already available. For the rest—sample swatches, colour cards. Signor Monti would check with the studio in Via della Spiga before they left in case they had anything there other than these. 'You are at the Garibaldi?'

'Of course. Just around the corner,' said Henry. 'I remember your studio.'

'The fountain?'

'Yes, but more the spaces behind locked doors, the courtyards.'

Signor Monti smiled. 'You like Milan, my friend.' It came out as 'my fren'. More intense somehow, more comradely. He gave a quick tug at a bolt of black shiny material. 'New,' he said stroking. 'Completely new fabric, with viscose. Manufactured in Germany for us exclusive.'

Henry took the slippery stuff in his hands, let it flow. 'Nice. Very nice. Can you guarantee one hundred per cent stability?'

'Of course.'

'And the colour range?'

Signor Monti lifted a finger. A man placed the appropriate swatch in his hand. Henry flicked through. 'No yellow?'

'Our designers have dispensed with yellow this year.'

'And the colour stability?'

'A hundred per cent also.'

They moved on to prices. Delivery dates. These of course must also be guaranteed. Signor Monti hedged. To Rufus, who had been watching the man with interest from the moment they met, he seemed to deflate slightly. 'Of course, of course.

But sometimes. You know how it is. One colour may be cancelled, another very popular. Otherwise of course, a hundred per cent, completely one hundred per cent.'

Henry nodded his head in silence. The follow-up, he had warned Rufus, can go wrong in Italy. The Japanese are more reliable in this respect.

Rufus was impressed. Henry undoubtedly knew his stuff. The excitement, the drama, even God help us the challenge, was obviously good for him. Adrenalin was pumping, which was just as well. They had two more factories to visit before returning to Milan.

They lunched together in the factory restaurant. Signor Monti looked carefully through the menu and ordered something which was not on it. Omelette. No tomato.

He asked after Martin Brown.

'Bad,' said Henry. 'Very bad, unfortunately. Ah, *farinata di ceci.*'

'What's that?' asked Rufus.

'Chickpeas and watercress.'

Rufus had risotto. It was not bad. Not bad at all.

He caught the Intercity to Prato early next morning. He activated his ticket in its yellow box, the use of which had been sussed out by Gaby. She was the perfect travelling companion; enterprising, delighted by success and undeterred by failure, she could push the world over on a good day. And she was good-natured, extraordinarily good-natured, considering. Poon Hill, for example. Amazing.

Rufus leaned back, stared at the bright blue netting and polished wood of the luggage racks, and thought about her. In his private dreams and fantasies she was his girlfriend. His best friend who was a girl and proved it daily.

In public she was his partner.

He enjoyed first-class travel. Even the temporary illusion

of wealth which came with Eurail had pleased him, where journeys end in lovers fighting and heaving packs and quick exits are essential in the battle for cheap accommodation within walking distance. Gaby had designed a system. She shot out of the first-class carriage like a rocket as the train reached the station. He guarded the packs, shoved them out the window and they were away laughing. They saw fellow backpackers off time after time, but the illusion of privilege had gone.

But this was real first class. First class with a suit and a briefcase. First class with class.

The carriage was not full. Rufus watched an elderly man seated across the aisle. A man as complete and unruffled as a handsome game bird. Such a perfect example of the species that Rufus stared from behind the cover of his paper, his gaze intent as a watcher's from a hide. What did he mean by complete? He tried to work it out. Secure in his own skin for starters. Rufus knew instantly several things about the man; his range and habitat, for example. This man was solid, wealthy, professional, well established in his own area and breeding ground. Nothing fly-by-night or migratory about him.

This man was in control, his life ordered. He had risen from a good night's sleep beneath one of those white feather duvets which really do work in winter and in summer unlike the el cheapos of home.

Does he have a wife or mistress? Does he lie alone? It is irrelevant. He has performed his ablutions, has been brisk in bathroom and lavatory, not puddling about for hours like Dad. He has shaved with a blade razor and how could you know that. You couldn't, but the smooth bloom of his unlined cheek gave the impression of close attention. Rufus felt his own chin. The man was not an electric razor user, that was for sure.

Cologne? Aftershave? Too far away to tell. He wore a suit of Prince of Wales check with hand-stitched lapels. Italian or

English? Henry would know. Rufus was getting keener every day on this clothes business. He was beginning to understand Henry's pain when the backs of ill-cut jackets pleated about the ears of seated TV politicians as they smiled into the camera and declined responsibility for mistakes which were theirs alone. The mute button wiped their excuses, the back slits strained over their departing bums. Shoddy, muttered Henry. Shoddy.

Rufus stared harder.

The old guy opens his briefcase and takes out a black diary tipped with gold edges which he consults gravely. He has gravity, this man. I could learn from him. He consults his watch, gold but not kitsch. By squinting with my better eye I can see that the numerals are Arabic. There is no call for Arabic numerals, I am told. People are perfectly happy with Roman. Except for me and the old guy, and he has found them. He can find what he wants. He has authority and presence and he is rich. He is complete. He is all of a piece, has been for years and will continue to be.

I slip my watch into my top pocket and move over to sit opposite him. 'Excuse me, sir,' I say, 'but do you speak English?'

He looks at me, well shaved and not pleased.

The accent is very slight. 'Yes.'

'Would you be kind enough to tell me the time?'

His face moves slightly, not a smile but not exactly a rejection. 'About two minutes later than when you removed your own watch.'

I laugh. What would you do. It's a bit late for touché. The ball stays in the silent court.

'Why did you want to speak to me?' he asks eventually.

I should have thought this through. I have acted on impulse. Shit.

I smile, lean forward. 'I wondered what line of business you are in. Just curiosity, ha ha.'

'I am Swiss,' he says, as though that explained something other than clean camping grounds and well-made clocks.

'Ah,' I say.

'And you?'

'New Zealand.'

'How extraordinary,' he says. 'What is your name?'

'Rufus Felton.'

He looks at me, a look both solemn and embarrassing—as though it's my fault, as though he has asked me to say grace before meat.

'Felton,' he says and leans back on the smart little first-class antimacassar thing, as white and crisp and complete as he is. 'I knew a Felton from New Zealand. His first name was Henry.'

I am delighted and show it. 'He's my father.'

'Good God,' he says and stares at my face as though he had to memorise it, take a photo, something. His eyes shut for a second.

'And may I ask what your . . .' (Your what? Business? Line? This man is not a captain of industry. He has his own firm. He is complete.) '. . . business is,' I say. I hear myself spluttering and turn it to a cough.

'I, too, am in the fashion industry.' He produces a card, gives it to me without a smile. 'Marco Grisoni. Perhaps your father will remember me. However, it was a long time ago.'

His eyes stay closed for some time. At last they open and he looks at me as though I might know something important.

'How old are you?'

'Thirty-five.'

He looks odd. Very odd indeed. '*O dio,*' he says.

'Are you returning to Milan?'

'Why do you ask?'

'Well, ah . . . I'm sure Dad would like to see you again.'

I'm not sure at all. There are not many people Dad wants to see again. I want to see this man again. This man interests me. I envy him. He has something I would like to have. He is old and he is Swiss and he is obviously tired, but he has got it made and I want to find out how he did it. What's more, I'm going to.

But I don't.

'I think not. Now if you will excuse me, Signor Felton, I have work to do, as I'm sure you do.'

'Yes, of course.'

The test of a champion, I read somewhere, is how he reacts in defeat. Tyson, it was. He hasn't been knocked out yet so it's hard to judge the true calibre of the man.

I smile at Signor Grisoni, shake his scarcely extended hand and return to my seat and read up on Enrico Baronti, my main man in Prato. His father's family, I read, came from Lucca, sixty miles north of Prato. So what. I remember not to sulk. Gaby taught me. The trick is to recognise you're doing it then stop. She can't stand sulkers. There are quite a lot of people Gaby can't stand. I think about Gaby, the way she walks, runs, her thin, quick wrists and ankles. I move on, fantasise you could call it, see her legs round my neck, my hands busy. Gaby is a sexy lady with a mind like a steel trap. She is all for one and I'm the one. What a team.

Enrico Baronti is what matters now.

Henry sat beside a naked plane tree in the small damp square near the hotel.

A small boy and his mother walked past hand in hand. In the other arm the boy carried, with care, a newly pressed black cloak, a Batman mask hung round his neck. They reached an appointed rendezvous near the swings. Small boys proliferated, Batman slipped into his cape and mask, Mamma twitched the sateen folds, wiped a wet park bench and sat smiling as the chase began. Batman, pursued by the forces of evil, headed for the open country. His cloak spun in the wind, muddy water splashed at his heels. Mamma applauded. Batman won. No one else had a chance.

'Hi,' said Rufus, sitting beside his father. 'What on earth are you doing in this grotty place?'

'I like wet trees,' said Henry. He indicated a breathless and triumphant Batman waving his mask above prostrate combatants. 'I was thinking, would the drama of that seem as interesting at home? As endearing?'

Rufus examined the sole of his shoe. 'I don't know.'

'Tell me about Prato.'

Triumph, total triumph. Rufus told him in detail, opened his briefcase, ran through figures, showed lists, demonstrated swatches. He had indeed done well and Henry told him so.

'Signor Baronti sent his greetings, best wishes, whatever.'

'Thank you.'

A larger boy was attempting to disrobe a now weeping Batman. Mamma lowered her head and charged.

'Look,' said Henry.

'What? Oh yeah. And I met another man you used to know. An old guy called Grisoni.'

'There are lots of Grisonis.'

'Marco Grisoni. He said it was years ago. About thirty.'

'More than that.'

'So you do remember.'

'Vaguely.'

'Tell me about him.'

Henry's head was spinning. 'There's nothing to tell.'

He leaned forward, put his head between his knees and breathed deeply.

'You okay?' said Rufus.

His father opened his eyes to find Batman crouched flat-footed in the mud before him, his head skewed upwards to peer at Henry's face. Mamma now carried the cloak, but the mask remained. The dark curls hung heavy, the eyes behind the mask were concerned. He pushed it back onto his forehead, an infant welder taking a break.

'*Il signore sta male!*' he said.

Mamma, flustered and voluble, tried to drag him away. Batman gave one shriek of fury and stayed rooted. Henry coughed, Rufus beat his back. Mamma panicked, tucked her son under one arm like a loaf and ran, trailing black sateen in dead leaves and dog shit.

The sound receded, echoing. '*Sta male, sta male!*'

'You okay?' said Rufus again.

'Yes, just a touch of dizziness. I've had rather an unsatisfactory day.'

Rufus relocked his briefcase.

'Unsatisfactory?'

'Yes.'

seven

Henry bought spring flowers from a florist near the hotel. Those mobile stalls outside the cemetery gates, stacked with cones of bright paper enclosing roses or a few carnations, always depressed him further. He wanted lots. Carla had been a generous woman.

He had first met her at a fashion show in 1960, one of those extravaganzas involving skittery little gold chairs beside a catwalk where elegant women glide in clothes designed to demonstrate the cutting skills, the flair, the vision of the maestro. Women so sleek they could enhance any garment however bizarre. Women swinging this way, that, a hand on a hip, a smile, a smoulder, a look-me-over and buy my wares which are not mine to sell. I am a clothes horse. I know my role among the inflated egos, the hard-nosed businessmen and women of the Milan fashion world and it is okay by me, buster, I can afford to dip my head, to slip from wool and retie silk. I demonstrate the genius of others.

I am essential to the cause. I am available for hire. I am expensive.

A hand jogged his elbow, champagne spilled, the woman apologised in Italian. As always, the speed defeated him. He mopped, she mopped, he promised lack of concern, she called for reinforcements, gave a peremptory tap on the shoulder of the man beside her, demanded handkerchiefs. The man turned, lifted uncomprehending palms as she snatched the silk one from his pocket and continued, voluble in her distress, her apologies, her horror.

Henry recognised him. He and Marco Grisoni had met through the years. They had smiled, shaken hands and forgotten each other until the next time.

Grisoni was now attempting to introduce the mopper, a process hindered by her efforts to return the now sodden rag to his breast pocket. He backed instinctively, gave a small bark of disgust.

Her laughter died. She held the handkerchief between thumb and finger for a second, dropped it and looked at Henry for the first time. 'Italian Swiss, *Signore*, have no sense of the ridiculous.'

Grisoni's expression did not change. 'Carla, may I present Signor Felton, my sister-in-law, Signora Grisoni.'

Henry bowed his head, opened his mouth to speak, was interrupted.

'Am I still your sister-in-law now Roberto is dead?'

'Yes.' Grisoni turned to Henry, made a small gesture indicating something. Embarrassment? Apology? 'My brother died last year.'

'I'm sorry.'

'Yes, it was very sad.'

They moved away, The woman placed her stiletto heel on the abandoned handkerchief, gave a swift grind and turned to smile. '*Arrivederci, signore.*'

His hotel bedroom had been stifling that September. No air conditioning, no air to condition. He tried the window again. It was jammed tight as it had been yesterday and for generations. So why so did he try. Because people do.

He turned on the television and flopped onto the bed. Black and white images came from Rome, Italian voices filled the narrow room.

He should take off his shoes. Didn't. Christ, it was hot.

The commentators became more excited as men stripped off tracksuits and lined up to race. Henry snapped upright at the black singlet and shorts. He leaned forward, willed himself to understand the rapid-fire Italian. Final—eight hundred metres. He'd made it this far, then, that promising young man they'd been on about at home. An Olympic finalist. Good luck to him. He would need it. It would be blazing hot there, the temperature, the tension from thousands of screaming fans.

Henry pulled off his tie, leaned nearer to help his man who was hopelessly boxed in. On the last bend, when the two leaders, a black man and a white, moved into their final sprint, a gap opened on the inner lane and the New Zealander surged through. Past the black man, past the white, past the lot to storm on down the last thirty metres and lunge for the line.

Henry was on his feet shouting. What a race, what a triumph, what a race. He flopped back exhausted. Snell, that was the name. Snell.

He was still standing as the flags rose, flopped back onto the bed as the band played 'God Save the Queen' not 'God Defend New Zealand'. But still the flag was there, too like the Australians' but up there at the right moment, flying on top of the world.

He sat beaming back at the shy grin, nodded as the head bent to receive the gold, then lay back.

He woke to another all black kit in the five thousand metre finals, another win. By eight metres, eight bloody metres! The slight figure of Halberg collapsed on his back and lay motionless.

Two gold medals. Who could he *tell*. This is patriotism, this is national pride, outdated jingoism, glory. What a fool

Marx must have been to think it could be forgotten for his higher cause.

Breathes there a man, with soul so dead,
who never to himself hath said,
This is my own, my native land!

Certainly not. Not Henry. Not Snell, not Halberg.

Christ in concrete, what a place it was. He was now striding around the narrow space available, banging his knees on the bed end, grinning his head off. He wanted to rush into the Monte Napoleone, grab men by the tie, women by the waist. Three million people, and two gold medals within hours. Listen, you clowns. Listen.

Breathes there a man. Even a man who had never run in his adult life, except for a bus.

He would ring Andy. Sometimes you have to and damn the expense.

Then he would get outside and walk, walk for miles.

He sat watching the waitresses in the café. He had been coming here for years, since the day when his halting Italian had resulted in a glass of warm sweetened milk instead of *caffelatte*. A nasty surprise, corrected immediately with laughing good humour. The two waitresses, there had never been more than two, worked harder than any male equivalent he had known except the French, and seemed a good deal happier. Henry liked everything about the place: the ornate double curve of the mahogany bar, the steaming indoor warmth in March, the crowded pavement tables now. The three-tiered chrome fruit-stand of oranges crowned with triumphant bananas pleased him. The six-foot fan-shaped light fittings, made from green bakelite in the days when it was a man-made miracle, continued to impress. Lit from behind and shimmering with iridescent greens, they sailed resplendent above din and clamour and laughter and grief.

The coffee was excellent.

But it was the waitresses who drew him back. They changed, of course, over the years, but every replacement seemed as efficient and insouciant as her predecessor. They appeared to be imbued with the pleasure of serving others.

He was in danger of getting sentimental about Italy. Rosa would love it. He would bring Rosa and the baby as soon as possible. The waitresses would be ecstatic. He had watched them yesterday, cooing with excitement over an immensely plain bambino in a pushchair, a solemn child with an overly large head and constant dribble.

The senior waitress brought more coffee. Her clinging bib-topped black trousers reminded him of a male gymnast's. They brought images of parallel bars, suspended rings and strength upside down. He saw himself sitting with Rosa, round as a ball on the sofa beside him as they had listened to the Olympic gymnastics the night before he left.

'To think there's people like him and people like me and we're both people. Don't you find that amazing?'

'He's not pregnant.'

She patted his arm. 'True.'

The waitress wore no bra beneath her long-sleeved T-shirt. Her breasts moved as she placed his coffee. These were not the chaste busts of virgin girls, these rounded shapes had made welcome, had given pleasure and probably sustenance. They were beautiful. Henry stirred in his seat. The strong brown face smiled into his. This was not flirting, or not the tentative backings and advancings of his salad days. This was lust for life, sheer joie de vivre. He swallowed and shifted again.

'Beautiful, aren't they?' said the woman at the table beside his.

His mouth dropped.

She nodded at the iridescent greens, the changing light of the plastic art deco fans above them.

'They are what bring me back.' She smiled. 'Don't look so surprised. We have met before.'

'We have?'

'I behaved badly and was dressed for it. Rossini's show. Carla Grisoni.'

'Of course.' She certainly looked different. Her black hair was no longer smoothed about her head. It hung loose and thick and heavy around a face strong-featured as that of the bosomed waitress, but less welcoming. Gold rings of various shapes circled each finger of her left hand and two on the right. She touched her chest. 'Today I am dressed casually.'

Well, yes.

She wore creased white trousers, a magenta top, white shoes and pink flowered socks. Her complexion was dark, her maroon lipstick appeared to be outlined with brown.

He told her about his countrymen's triumphs.

She turned a hand palm upwards on the table. '*Bravissimi*,' she said.

He changed the subject. Did she live near here?

No, she was on her way to the Brera. She was interested in art. But in Italy art has a capital A. She was not interested in capitals. Her English was fluent and idiomatic, she was quick-witted and made him laugh. There was something vaguely subversive about her. Contradictory. Her ridiculous flowered socks and shapeless trousers did not match carefully shadowed eyes and crafted lips.

The shape of her thighs against the jersey was distinctly haunch-like, he noticed as they rose to leave. She was not overly thin.

She turned to him on the pavement and gave him her hand. '*Arrivederci, signore*.' She paused. 'On second thoughts, would you like to accompany me to the Brera? I want to check up on the Saint Sebastians.'

'In what way?'

'The number of arrows. I keep a list.'

Her mind operated in an unusual way. She was an unusual woman.

They walked quickly through hot crowded streets. The temperature, according to a street clock, was 30°C. She refused a taxi. 'I walk everywhere.'

'That's unusual, isn't it? For an Italian woman. In this heat?'

'I am French, French, French. I was foolish enough to marry young. A Swiss.' The words withered in the stale air. 'Italian Swiss. The worst sort.'

You have to say something. Henry tried compassion. 'And he died?'

'Last year. And his brother blames me. Your friend Marco Grisoni.'

'I knew he was suspect,' he said.

She turned to him and laughed loudly, a laugh so unexpected, so all encompassing that he laughed back. They stood united by mirth and friendliness, laughing at what? Censure? Smugness? Heartbreak? He felt an unexpected tightening, a kick of desire.

'Quick,' she said, 'let's get inside. At least it will be cooler inside. Their precious Art works.' She nodded at barricades and shutters and rubble nearby, at large signs saying *In restauro*. 'The whole of Italy is *in restauro*. It never stops.'

'You buy the tickets,' she said as they entered. 'You must improve your Italian.'

'Where are you come from, *Signore*?' asked the guard.

'New Zealand.'

A clutch of small boys being marshalled and shuffled into Art by a distracted nun stopped in their tracks. 'New *Zee*land.' They demonstrated rucks, tackles, a mini scrum. Yelled wow, gee, hang, in Italian, and punched the air. 'All Blacks,' they shouted. Henry was tempted to tell them his good news. Snell, he would demonstrate to their blank upturned faces, Halberg. Vroom, vroom. But the nun had regained control and they disappeared.

'Do you like children?' she asked.

'I hope so. My wife is pregnant.'

She sighed. 'One's own one can love. Just.'

A provoking woman, his mother would have called her. He didn't have to play. There would be no knowing glances, no smiling collusion.

'Good,' he said.

She gave a dismissive shrug. 'I apologise. I was being . . . What is the word in English?'

'Glib.'

'Glib?'

'A cheap crack. Facile.'

No use. Worse if anything. She turned away, her head drooped, her hair fell forward.

He took her arm. 'Come and tell me about the paintings.'

She was informative and unpatronising, knowledgable and fun. She led him gently, as presumably the nun would now be leading the rugby fans. She assumed nothing.

Yes, she had remembered correctly about Saint Sebastian's arrows. The saint gazed heavenwards above the five arrows in his beautifully modelled torso, his face pained but calm.

They moved on to a triptych. Saint Jerome's lion appeared in each panel like a large and hairy dog; hiding ineffectually behind a tree while monks fled in terror, looming from the shadows in the saint's candle-lit study, flattened with grief beside his master's laid-out corpse, he was faithfulness incarnate.

'I like the backgrounds best,' she said before a fifteenth-century Madonna and Child. 'They are the parts where the artist could let go, be free to explore, be true to his own vision, even if it's only blue castles and misty hills. To tell the truth. Do you know the work of Louise Bourgeois?'

'No.'

Her face was stern. 'A French sculptor. She lives in America now. Even photographs of her work are not easy to find. It is wonderful. Strong. As true, as honest, as pissing.'

Women in Meadowbank did not speak of pissing to strangers, male or female. They did not speak of pissing at all. They went to the bathroom and they shut the door. At picnics they sought a generous bush.

She was sending him signals he found hard to believe.

'What do you mean?'

'It wasn't Saint Sebastian's arrows.' She brushed them away. 'An excuse.'

He stared around the high well-lit walls, noted the exit on the right, gave himself time. The nun was now telling her team about the Piero della Francesca, explaining which figure was the donor and why he was in the picture. And, she asked their stiffening boredom, could anyone see an ostrich egg in the picture? Could anyone see *l'uovo*?

Sì! Sì! Any fool could see. The big fellow hanging above the head of the blessed Virgin.

'And what is the meaning, the significance of this egg, children?'

Total silence from all.

'I don't understand you,' said Henry finally.

Legs apart, arms at the ready, her smile crooked and accusing, she disagreed. 'Now you are lying.'

'No one is lying, we are just playing games. If you ask me to do a Saint Sebastian count with you and I agree we don't have to fuss about arrows or truth or you or me. You make things too difficult for yourself. Slow down. Relax.'

'You sound like Marco.'

'Why do you dislike him so much?'

'He pursues me like a dog and always has. He was glad when his brother died.'

Again that feeling of instability, that trembling shift. He thought of Rosa. Stopped. Felt himself ache for the woman beside him.

'He thought he could get me more easily. Have me like the bitch he thinks me.'

'Oh, for God's sake.' His palms flung apart. 'I don't want to hear all this. Why are you telling me?'

'Because you are a stranger.'

'I am married and my wife is pregnant.'

'The first?'

'Yes.'

She glanced at her fingernails. 'First,' she murmured.

'And will probably be the last. Rosa has problems.'

'Now you are telling me. "Rosa has problems." Sad. I am sad to hear it.' She put a hand up and turned his chin, stared into his eyes. 'What harm can a friendship with an unknown woman do to your Rosa ten thousand miles away, pregnant or not pregnant? Logically speaking, friendship with a woman is more understandable in a man when his wife is pregnant. Psychologically also.'

'And emotionally?' he snapped.

'Goodbye,' she said. She held out her hand for him to kiss.

His lips met metal, brushed gold. 'Carla.'

She slipped her arm through his as they walked on. 'The exit is this way.'

The nun was now tackling perspective. The small boys sat cross-legged before Mantegna's *Dead Christ*. They had perked up a little and sat hunting for wounds. One was missing. 'Sister, sister, where is the one in the side?'

'It is hidden, Piero. I have explained to you. Why is the wound in the body of Christ hidden, class?'

Silence.

'Because of perspective. All is not seen. I have told you this before.'

The Milan Lions Club had restored a twelfth-century Madonna and Child near the entrance. Good on them. Good.

They became lovers that night.

All day in Prato he had felt alternately weak at the knees or walking on air, his longing tamped with tenderness or overheated. Had he felt like this eight years ago with Rosa. Of course. Of course not. Of course.

Trees were visible above the balustrade of the roof garden opposite as he ran down the steps from the hotel. The sense always present in Milan of lives hidden from view, of seclusion behind locked doors and courtyards, seemed stronger than ever. Milan does not lie back and welcome. She has to be sought out. Entrée is required.

He pressed the button on the brass entry plate of the high stone wall. Carla's voice answered. The door opened into a cobbled courtyard. He walked past a statue of a boy holding a cornucopia trickling rusty water, turned left past unmown grass, lemon trees and large urns, into a walled garden. Rosa had a thing about secret gardens. She had kept her childhood copy of the book for the baby.

Carla ran to meet him laughing, skipping the rough patches, her hands stretched wide.

She had moved into the studio flat after Roberto died. She wanted to get away from all that *dolce vita* rubbish. She wanted to work and she wanted to live where she worked and she was delighted to be able to greet him where she worked and after they would go around the corner to the Girarrosto Restaurant which was not to be missed, and reasonable as well. When they were completely restored they could return for more love. 'Is that plan good?'

'Very good.'

Milan is made for love, she told him. For secrecy, intrigue, corruption and love. What more could he want. What more could he possibly want.

Very little at the time.

She licked his ear. 'Do you like chickpeas?'

'I don't know.'

'Chickpea fritters with watercress. *Farinata di ceci.* Very delicious. Very restorative. Lombardy's answer to the onion soup of France.'

He did not remember much about her studio. Just that it was astonishing, that he had never seen anything like it; swatches, patterns, design sketches, cards of buttons and metres of trim lay all around. There was a large coloured poster of Sophia Loren photographed against a red background, her face resting on a velvet sofa. Her mouth was fractionally open, her smile intimate and amused, her enormous eyes wide with welcome.

'Why on earth?' he asked.

'Because she is the most beautiful woman in the world and she knows it and she can still laugh. She can laugh at herself and at men also. Can love and laugh and break your heart. She is life. Life and love and death and despair.' Carla kissed her hand to the smile.

'Many Italians have photographs of the Pope. She is my Pope. I dropped the other one when I grew up. Shall I tell you?'

He nodded.

'There is a memorial in our town in France. One in every town, every village, always inscribed the same: *A ses morts glorieux.* Twenty-one dead in the last war and our town is small.' She demonstrated size with her fingers. 'But it was the *victimes civiles* that decided me. "Killed by the Gestapo—one; killed by the resistance—one; deported—four; *interné politique*—one; *défence passive*—one." All those killings, all those factions. God couldn't make up his mind. He saved no one.' She lifted an arm to her friend: 'Life is better.'

She was as extravagant as her studio, as lavish as the green fanned lights.

He was never entirely sure what she did, or rather which of her many activities was the most important to her. She had worked for five years as Rossini's assistant. She loved him dearly and he drove her insane. Never had she seen such nerves. She now worked closely with textile manufacturers and sometimes designed collections for them. She had been known to design printed scarves of great beauty. *Stampa personalizzata*. She was interested in detail. The right button could make or mar.

She taught him a great deal. 'A grey deal,' his father had said; why, Henry had never asked. Many things he had never asked and many things were unanswerable. Why, for example, could he tolerate the possibility of Carla's future unfaithfulness with comparative equanimity, when the same thought with regard to Rosa reduced him to gibbering panic.

It was not that he loved Carla less. He loved her passionately, loved her body and her large crooked smile and the way her back arched to meet him. Her unexpectedness, her body and her soul.

And he loved Rosa. His love who could deliver. His wife in bed and out.

It was all very odd. Ridiculous, even, he thought in his bleaker moments. Here he was behaving like some airborne version of the mariner in *Captain's Paradise* flying from the arms of his exotic mistress to the suburban felicity of his loving wife. And back.

*

He arrived home a month before Rufus was born. It was a difficult birth. Toxaemia. There would be no more babies.

And no letters from Milan, of course. That had been agreed on. He would return twice a year. He would be back regularly. To work; to work-related expenses and his work-related love.

Her variousness never faltered. She could slip from proud elegance to street-kid charm with only the lop-sided tug of her grin in common.

Her emotions appeared to work in similar fashion. She swung from hypo- to hyper-sensitive, from action to languor, from rage for the world to rage against it. Her pleasure in sex and his company appeared constant.

He could never understand why she asked so little of him. She made occasional snide remarks about Rosa and the child, but very few. 'Rufus! *Cristo*. No one can be called Rufus.'

'My son is.'

She had more luck with her contempt for anything pertaining to New Zealand. 'Don't ever talk about it. Not a word.'

He let it pass. Patriotism, like guilt, was suspended.

He came, they loved, he left. And he came again. Do not forget that. He came again and again and again.

He should have felt guilty about Rosa and wondered why he didn't. There seemed little point. Not a grey deal.

He and Carla fought occasionally throughout the years. Once or twice she had refused to meet him at first, but such occasions were rare. Mostly he remembered not rows but a kind of teasing banter; irrelevant opportunities pounced upon to belittle his background and education.

Cows, for example, at the café where she sat eating ricotta and jam. She was in elegant mode, her smooth black hair swept into a roll up the back of her head, her lipstick darker than ever. She put down her spoon with a small decisive click and nodded at the heavy gilt-framed oil on the wall above them.

Cows were ambling home to be milked. Or he assumed they were. Like the *Dead Christ*, all was not revealed, but the bonneted maiden had a switch in her hand. They must be going somewhere.

'That painting is *inglese*.'

'How do you know?'

'Sunbonnets. No Italian or French milkmaid would ever have worn such a thing. Never.'

'But look at the cows. Totally French. Huge, raw-boned, terrifying. These are not English cows. Nor New Zealand. Not the cows of Home.'

It was a game ritualised by use; a gentle stirring, a stoke-up. She lead with her chin.

'With a capital H presumably?'

'Of course.'

'Those are not French cows.'

'They're certainly not New Zealanders. Nothing rangy about ours. Neat and sleek. Brindled velvet. I'll send you a postcard.'

'Of *cows*.'

'It wouldn't all be cows. The cows would be incidental, browsing around the foothills of snow-capped mountains, ambling through scenic wonderlands.'

'And hot pools,' she snapped.

The thought appalled him, the agonised bellows, the pain. 'God forbid.'

'A terrible place. Even the cows lack direction.'

'It was you who consigned them to the hot pools.'

'Me! Never!'

Ridiculous. Idiotic. And memorable in every detail.

The worst times were always after they had met Marco Grisoni. These occasions; in the interval at La Scala, at fashion shows throughout the years and, one particularly disastrous time, on the train from Como, always followed the same pattern. Icy greetings, flaunting ridiculous over-the-top behaviour from Carla, chill composure from Marco and inept bumbling goodwill from himself. No, not goodwill, never that, he disliked the man and always had, and if a fraction of Carla's stories about him were true, had every reason so to do; but something akin to it, something placatory, a social hypocrisy, an attempt to smooth.

It was his behaviour more than the chill calm of Grisoni himself which fired Carla to rage whenever they left the man's presence. Rage at Henry.

What had he done?

Nothing! That was the point. He had done nothing. He had crawled, he had compromised, he had *accommodated* the man.

Despair followed later. 'Even Giacomo, my own son, he turns my own son against me. Woos him. Lies to him. Money, money, money. He promises him the moon and lies about me. At his age, so young. Nine, ten. All lies.'

It was only at these times that she mentioned her son. He was at boarding school.

'Isn't that rare in Italy?'

'No.'

A letter addressed to the warehouse arrived on his desk in August 1980. It was a long letter, loving and elegiac and final. She was about to remarry. For security, she explained, and he believed her. And loneliness. Twenty years was a long time to be a mistress. Too long.

He agreed, he understood, he wept. He never saw her again.

Giacomo Grisoni's letter had arrived six years ago. His mother, Carla, had died. She had left instructions that Signor Felton was to be informed. Her death had been sudden and painless.

Her husband had been away when she was taken ill but fortunately Giacomo and his uncle Marco had been at her bedside when she died. Last rites had been administered.

Giacomo would be grateful if Signor Felton did not communicate further with him in any way, either now or in the future.

Henry left the office and walked, headed for the harbour bridge and turned back to search the envelope yet again. She must have sent him some letter, some words, a note. Something. The son had not sent it on. Henry would write for it immediately, demand it. No, he wouldn't. He would seek him out next autumn and tear him apart. He would get his rightful letter.

When he came to his senses again he realised she would not have written him one, even if she had had time. It would not have been right. Not true. She was a married woman.

Henry walked towards the Cimitero Monumentale with the bunch of flowers hanging head downwards in his hand. He did not come every time but was glad when he was able to, when it worked out, when he could think about Carla and nothing else, could stand in that cold crowded place and climb the ladder to leave the flowers in the vase attached to the front of her tomb. Could climb down again to get into the open air and wish for the thousandth time that she had been buried outdoors. That he could have stood by her graveside and thought. And what difference, what conceivable difference could it have made to those haphazard ramblings where she was buried.

It was better to visit the cemetery during the week. In the weekend, especially on Sundays, the chattering crowds, the queue for ladders and long-spouted watering cans, the general air of camaraderie, of people with a shared purpose going about their business, polite and helpful to each other as holidaymakers in the communal kitchen of a camping ground, reduced him to either despair or hysteria.

What could you remember up a ladder when there was a queue waiting? Would the flowers fit in the container? My lover, my dead love.

The sight of the Cimitero Monumentale itself always gave him pause. It was aptly named, the scale enormous as were the monuments. Five vast tombs adorned with grieving marble forms stood on the balustrades of balconies on three sides of a building adjoining a piazza large enough for a military rally, for a display of armoured might, an exhortation from Il Duce in his heyday. Death, Cimitero Monumentale believed, would have no dominion.

It began to rain as he arrived. Small gentle rain, coming, if he'd got it right, from the west.

Christ, if my love were in my arms

And I in my bed again.

Yes. Well. Thank God Rufus was in Prato.

He put out a hand to open the gate. It was locked.

He glanced around, noted the absence of flower stalls, the lack of people and finally, the large sign. *Chiuso.*

A small man in a cap moved forward from an attendant's booth inside the iron railings. He was sympathetic but cheerful. '*Chiuso*,' he explained, '*Chiuso a tutti.* Cleansing, cleansing.'

Grazie, grazie.

Prego.

Not at all. Shoulders slumped, Henry turned to the right. He knew where to go. He lifted the flowers and held them upright. It was not the man's fault. He should have checked. Everything requires cleansing.

Carla's remains were interred in the lower level of the right-hand wing of the building, in a storage system set in stone.

He found what he was looking for—a large fan-shaped

window, or rather crescent-shaped hole in the wall divided by iron struts, which looked down the length of the wing. Individual tombs lined the entire length of the area from top to bottom. From the footpath he was at eye level with the uppermost tombs and the row of large globe lights that ran from one end of the space to the other. Long ladders, flowers artificial and real, all were in position. It was well lit. He could read the inscriptions of the tombs nearest, a Giacomo, a baroness, a Lucia. He could see the photographs, a miniature sculpture of a child. Carla, he knew, was further along. Her inscription brief.

Carla Françoise Stephani 1933–1990.

Nothing more. No husband, no child. Nothing.

Henry stood watching. Cleansing was indeed in progress. A motorised scrubber wielded by one man was making loud slurping sounds on the wet marble. It was followed by a man pushing a large mop attached to a huge red bucket on wheels. Cheerful and safe as a child's toy, it trundled in front of him as he sang loudly and tunefully. '*Your tiny hand,*' he roared, '*is frozen.*'

Henry leaned his head against the wet railings. Rain fell. He straightened, undid the complicated restraining ribbons and wires around the flowers and pushed paper whites, jonquils, daffodils and freesias through gaps in the struts. He hoped the singer would pick up these offerings from on high, would share them with the scrubbing operator, would delight their wives or sweethearts. For you my beloved, *con espressione*.

But perhaps they were in retreat, had finished this end.

Oh Christ—*Cristo*.

It had stopped raining. He walked back to the hotel, a long, cold, mindless walk. He had reached the park near the hotel and Batman and his dresser before he had another thought, one he could have shared with Carla and no one else in the world. The man with the bucket could have been a Nellie Lutcher fan, could have been singing with the same gusto and emotion the Italian version of *Hurry on down to my house, baby.*

'Hey, look,' said Rufus. 'There's Signor Grisoni. Who's the guy with him?'

Henry chewed a mussel and glanced. 'I've no idea.'

He chewed harder, looked again and saw that he had lied. That face, that simian charm, that male version of Carla must be a relative. Or, God help him, her child. Giacomo would be about ten years older than Rufus. It fitted. Henry's gut tightened. He felt weak, dizzy, not well.

Rufus's look was stern. 'What's the matter?'

Henry lied with more purpose. 'I don't like the look of him. Tell me more about Prato.'

'There's nothing more to tell. And why have we come to a French restaurant in Milan?'

'Someone recommended it.' Henry heard his own voice pitched too high. 'Rufus, there's something I feel I should tell you. Something about Uncle Andy.'

Rufus dragged his eyes away from Marco Grisoni and his bright-eyed friend; a dynamic character, voluble, obviously a good talker.

'What on earth? He's been dead forever.'

It was not crassness. Henry knew it was not. Nor disrespect. It would have been better left unsaid.

'Thirty years.'

'More. I was two. Bee gave me a Dinky.'

'Listen,' said his father and told him. He spoke fluently and well as he used Andy's death and probable despair as a diversionary activity. He took occasional sneak looks at Grisoni and his nephew. Grisoni senior had not seen them or, even better, he had seen them and chosen to ignore them while

Henry discussed the sexual predilections and likely suicide of his long dead brother with his inattentive son.

Rufus glanced at his newly delivered plate. 'I thought *fromage de tête* would be brains.'

'No, potted meat, brawn.'

'Bugger,' said Rufus mildly. He put out a hand to his father. 'Dad, do you mean to say you've been fussing about this for over thirty years? I don't mean his death, that's tragic, sure. But a) you'll never know whether or not it was deliberate, not for sure, and b) who would give a stuff about fetishism?'

'This was in 1962.'

'So?'

They never understand, the young. How can they. They weren't there.

'He and Bianca were going to be married. She screamed and roared and sent him packing.'

Rufus was silent for a moment. He considered the evidence. With the certainty of youth, the superiority of those who were not there and don't know, who saw-by-the-paper and know what they think, he considered the evidence and came down on the wrong side.

'Yeah, well. If she saw him at it. Bit of a shock, I suppose. Might put her off.' He paused. 'Still.'

'Still. As you say.'

'It doesn't seem enough to make him top himself.'

'For God's sake, man! It would have killed our father. He was . . .' What would you say, Henry, what would you say. Bigoted. Terrified of difference. Idiotic. 'He was very conservative.'

Rufus was watching the Grisonis, admiring a bit of napkin play; the uncle touching each corner of his mouth, the nephew mopping with enthusiasm. 'Ah,' he said.

Henry looked at him bleakly. So that's it then. The conversation is over.

'You've got brawn on your face,' he said.

Rufus mopped. 'Why tell me now?'

'I thought you might be grateful to know.'

'Oh shit, Dad. I mean about Andy.'

'Bianca knows,' said Henry.

'So?'

'And she also knows that you sent your mother several pairs of shoes.'

Rufus smiled that sweet smile which is rare in men but not unknown. The smile a patient and indulgent parent might give to a child who insists on doing up its own shoes when it can't and the whole thing is going to take hours. 'So what's the problem, Dad?'

Henry was getting angry. 'Your mother does not know about Andy being different. Bianca will tell her and she will worry that it is some hereditary defect.' Get it, thicko? Straight shooting from the old dugout. Get it?

'Memo,' burped Rufus. 'Never have *fromage de tête* again.' He leaned forward to explain, 'Dad, just because there's one, how shall I say, oddball in the family, doesn't mean there's going to be a genetic trickle-down. And who cares? Not me. Certainly not Gaby. She's got a very healthy libido.'

The lingo, the smugness, even the non sequitur infuriated Henry further. And why is it always 'healthy'. Any moment soon it will be 'serious'. A seriously healthy libido, after which there will be nowhere left for it to go other than to slide into a problem. My partner has a seriously healthy libido problem. Jesus wept.

Rufus, undeterred by his previous reception from Signor Grisoni, was on his feet. 'Come on, Dad. Let's go and say hi to Grisoni and his offsider.'

'No!'

'Why on earth not?' said Rufus over his shoulder.

Henry watched in panic. 'Hi' was not a greeting for this

over-priced French restaurant, and there were certainly no offsiders. People met by appointment and no one had made an appointment for him to meet the only child of his deceased mistress, a man who had told him in writing that he had no wish for further communication between them ever again.

He wiped his sweating hands on his trouser legs and followed his son.

Grisoni and his nephew stood and greeted them with composure. Grisoni invited them to join him for a brandy. Henry, who could see how much the man was enjoying the situation, thanked him and asked for a double. They were introduced to Giacomo, a man in his forties, charming, friendly and open. No, he was not part of the fashion world. He was a banker. Milan had more banks per capita than any other city in the world. Did Signor Felton know this?

'Yes,' said Henry.

Rufus, on the other hand, did not. This was fascinating. This was one of the most interesting things Rufus had heard for some time. He and Giacomo talked in English. They did more than that, they exchanged details of their working life, they compared notes, they yarned. Grisoni senior and Henry watched them in silence.

Marco Grisoni had not changed much throughout the years. Sleeker but not fatter, balder but not bald. Eventually he leaned forward, touched Giacomo's jacket. 'Signor Felton knew your mother, Giacomo.'

Calm as Lake Como in sunshine, Henry found his voice. 'A long time ago.'

'How long ago would it be now since you met?' said Grisoni smiling.

'Over thirty years,' said Henry.

Again that smile. 'Thirty-five I think.'

'That'd be right,' said Rufus. 'I remember Mum telling me you got back the month before I arrived.'

Grisoni junior stiffened. His shape, his whole personality tightened, focused—stared in disbelief. '*That* one?' he gasped.

What is going on here? Something is undoubtedly going on in this uptight place which was recommended by some airhead.

Grisoni senior is playing Dad like a trout in the Tongariro. Dad is hooked, beached at the feet of the scurrying waiters, the trays, the half-eaten fromage de fucking tête. He slumps in his chair, stares eyeball to eyeball at Grisoni senior.

Grisoni junior also appears to be in some sort of shock.

'Yes,' says his uncle. 'Thirty-five exactly.'

Dad stands. 'We must be going, Rufus.'

Giacomo Grisoni is on his feet. 'Surely not, your brandy half drunk? I must hear more. Memories of my mother, you understand, are so precious. Tell me more, please *Signore*.'

But it's the way he says it. I can feel it in the crotch. The guy has turned to ice. '*Epée ou pistolet?*' We had it in French.

Giacomo smiles at his uncle. Dad doesn't see this but I do. Marco drops one eyelid in a half-wink. Giacomo stares at him, still questioning, still not able to believe. He is mouthing something, some query.

Marco Grisoni gives the smallest possible nod.

Giacomo swings an astonished hand sideways and knocks over Dad's brandy. It sweeps outwards, a brown stain seeping to the edge of the stiff white cloth.

'No,' says Dad. 'I'm afraid we must go.'

Grisoni senior bows. 'Of course,' he says. 'We must detain you no longer.'

No one shakes hands.

So what's going on? Gaby would know.

'What was all that about, Dad?' I say in the cab.

'Grisoni's a thug and always has been.'

'I quite liked him.'

'Where did you meet him?'

'I told you. On the way to Prato. In the train.'

'Oh yes. The train.'

Dad closes his eyes. Blue, red, pink lights from the neon ads swing around, lie across our knees in stripes, day glo Dad's hair.

'You know,' I say, 'when we first arrived here I remember being surprised that taxis were called taxis. Nuts, eh?'

His eyes open. 'Yes,' he says. 'Not very bright.'

eight

The man at the tip told her he'd have to let her in free if she came many more times. Pleased by goodwill, Rosa grinned back. Better a job here than at the tip face; driving the bulldozer, the stench would stay with you, but here with the pines and the gulls whirling and a little row of salvaged items for sale—a pushchair, a suspect-looking heater, a cot—a man could be his own boss. Presumably he had a heater of his own in his hut; a kettle, sandwiches. And always the chance of a saleable find.

Rufus had had a student job at the domestic waste disposal unit in Otahuhu. The guys there, he said, had it made. The first one started his lunch-hour at ten and the last at three in the afternoon. They bolted their pie or whatever and spent the rest of the hour scanning the incinerated remains of the waste for treasure as it travelled past their eyes on its way to eventual resurrection as garden compost. If they found anything it was theirs. And the stuff they found! Diamond rings, bracelets, watches, money. It was understandable, but Rufus just hadn't thought about it before. A lot of the trove was useless, of course, false teeth, glass eyes, things of that nature. Still. It would add interest and the odds would be better than Lotto.

He didn't get a go. It was a perk for the permanents.

Rosa drove on and unloaded the trailer, her arms tugging, her eyes down for nails and sharp edges. The circling gulls landed, inspected briefly and wheeled high in disgust. This was non-biodegradable refuse, real dump stuff: ragged lengths of mouldy scrim, layers of dead wallpaper, pile after pile of newspapers. The sad and sorry mess of a life which had abandoned order, or been forced to admit defeat; had been unable to clean and maintain, or had got sick of it. Had run out of puff.

Despite her former enthusiasm for her role, Rosa knew how the previous owner had felt. The disposal of inorganic refuse is essential, yes indeed, but repetitive. She had hoped that her job in the triumvirate would be more exciting, would involve spells of action at the sharp end; of hacking, biffing, tearing apart like Bianca in borrowed overalls, or Gaby in a back-to-front baseball cap running up and down ladders shouting. Rosa's job was to load the trailer, drive to the tip, unload and return for more. She was beginning to realise that the catharsis of tip visits occurs only when you're getting shot of the fruits of your own labours, the mountain of your prunings, the waste of your years.

It was not the physical effort involved. She was strong as a Shetland pony, and would continue to be so as the years rolled by and the tall and languid wilted about her.

Her main source of job satisfaction was her minor skill in backing the trailer. It's not easy backing a trailer, quite an art, in fact. But after a few days she was bored; was tired of the dust and the red nose, the snorting discomfort and the head like a pumpkin. The muck and muddle of it all, the carting and the dumping.

'I think,' she said, as they sat eating her egg sandwiches in the derelict back garden, 'that we should take turns doing different jobs. I'd like to have a turn at stripping scrim.'

Bianca and Gaby chewed more slowly, stared at her solemn as two cows which had followed her across a paddock at Pukekohe last week, had stopped when she stopped, had moved on when she did; silent, attentive and puzzled. What was she up to now.

'Why?' said Bianca finally.

'I think it would be more fun. More . . . more meaningful.'

'You find the tip meaningful. You said so.' Gaby stretched, brushed away a passing bee from the buddleia. 'This stuff stinks.'

'I said it was cathartic.'

'Same difference.'

'Catharsis is emotional release, a purging. Not . . .'

'From the dump you get this?'

Again that feeling of unease, of unexpected slants and angles to words which seemed to characterise her conversations with Gaby. 'What I meant was . . .'

Bianca was not having this nonsense. 'Of course you can't do anything else, Ros. You're too short.'

'*We're the flowers in your dustbin*,' screamed a male voice next door.

'Sex Pistols. The guy's a nerd,' said Gaby and chewed again.

'And besides,' Bianca glanced at her, 'can you drive a trailer?'

'No,' said Gaby.

Bianca brushed her fingers, 'Well, there you are.'

Rosa stood up, stowed thermoses and let them have it. She was sorry to have to remind them but she had had enough. Henry and, by extension, herself were paying for this enterprise, totally, one hundred per cent and happy to do so for the common weal. Weal, she said again. If anyone was a partner in this enterprise, she was and in future she wished to be treated as one. If she wanted to strip wallpaper or hessian she would do so. And furthermore, someone else, she said, glancing around the still, enclosed space, the bees, the buddleia, the quiet, someone else could make the sandwiches tomorrow.

Having stood up and stowed, there seemed nowhere else to go. Sauntering was impossible. She scrambled across rubble to the rampant banksia rose.

Bianca and Gaby watched her rear. 'But who will drive the trailer, Ros?' said Bianca.

'*Flow-ers*,' yelled the voice.

Gaby said nothing. She couldn't stand people who sulked and when the hell was Roof coming home. This lot was getting to her. She looked at Rosa's behind upended over a pile of junk, her hands tearing at grass and weeds. Nuts.

She lit a cigarette, offered Bianca one. Bianca held up her own packet. Justin had not liked women smoking, let alone a wife. Gaby handed her lighter, was thanked.

The sun shone.

Rosa's mind was busy. She would stop and get her work gloves, any moment she would do that. It was ridiculous to be doing this bare-handed; there might be glass, twisted wire, anything beneath this choking weed, dangerous refuse awaiting transportation to an alternative site which had never been offered.

Who drives the trailer. *Who pays the piper.* And what on earth does that mean. Henry was quite right. They don't make sense, these old saws. None of them makes sense. Upended, flustered and breathing fast, she felt a surge of affection for Henry, who understood that all we know is that we don't know a thing. Not really. Just snatches. A glimpse, here and there.

She would stop this petulance, this rage, ignore this ridiculous sense of isolation and exclusion. Would stop snivelling into Wandering Jew and was that racist.

Perhaps Granny F had got it right. The thought depressed her. Mrs Felton had explained her real reason for going to

Pukekohe after her husband died. Had explained quietly and calmly to Rosa in her bedroom as they packed her 'personal belongings' before the packers arrived. 'I suppose they mean my knickers,' she said. 'Very wise. Old women's smalls would frighten the wits out of those heroes.'

She stood small, spry and neat as a pin. Her long white hair had been cut the year before when she broke her arm and could no longer cope with a bun. She was a walking oxymoron, a geriatric Peter Pan. Rosa opened her mouth to tell her and shut it. Even someone as ruthlessly clear-sighted as Mrs Felton might not be flattered.

Her bedroom was unlike any other Rosa had seen. Mrs Felton slept alone and had done since Henry was a child. Plain as a nun's cell, the room was whitewashed and minimalist fifty years before the style caught on. The furniture consisted of a narrow wooden bed, a kauri chest, a table and a chair. There were no pictures and only one black and white photograph in a leather frame on the table; a young man in uniform smiled, his cap on the slant, his pipe in his hand. Her brother Ian had been killed as a sub-lieutenant in the *Neptune*.

Rosa and Henry had tried to explain that it would be better for Mrs Felton to stay in town. They had not put it like that. You didn't tell Mrs Felton what would be better for her. She already knew. And they could scarcely have said it would be more fun. They had appealed to her pragmatism, had said it would make sense if they had found her a small flat or house nearby. They had not said, where they could keep an eye on her. They had more sense. You don't keep eyes on stoics. They might catch you at it.

So there would be no more popping in, no hot soup on the wing, no easy closeness with a woman Rosa admired. She would miss her.

Packing pink bloomers, she made one last try. 'Gran, why are you going all the way out there?'

'All the way? About thirty miles.' Mrs Felton finished folding a spencer, laid it with its fellows and sat down on her bed. Rosa remembered her faint surprise. Admittedly there was nowhere else to sit, but Mrs Felton did not sit on beds.

'I'll tell you the real reason, Rosa. Don't tell Henry. He wouldn't understand.' She paused. 'On second thoughts I think he might and that would be worse.' She picked up the fringe of the white cotton bed cover, ran it through her fingers. 'I have decided that I don't like people, people in general. I never have particularly, not the whole world. Some, yes, a few, but by and large I prefer my own company.' She gave what Henry called her honk. 'Don't look so worried. I was never gregarious. It must have been hard for Henry's father, a mismatch all round. But now I find I dislike too many, women in particular, so it seems sensible to go where I won't have to see them—other than family and by appointment. And I like the country, the life. Pukekohe will do very well.' She smiled Rufus's smile. 'Don't you find women trying?'

The playcentre young mothers, the good friends, the laughs. 'No, not at all.'

'Perhaps you're right. But there are too many rogue humming birds about for me. Flutterers. Women dripping syrup which turns to acid. Enchanting creatures, but the sting comes later.'

'You don't understand,' said Rosa, 'Bianca doesn't . . .' Mrs Felton brushed Bianca away.

'Devious women. Older women on the whole, but by no means always. Retailers of chit and chat who don't say what they think, don't mean what they say, don't ask what they want to know.' She paused. 'Though give them their due, it might be a difficult question. "Did your son kill himself? And if so why?" That's what lies behind their whispers, their turned heads, their intrusive smiles.'

There must be something to say, something not entirely

banal. Rosa couldn't find it. 'They don't mean to,' she bleated.

'Then why do they do it? I do not *require* such women.'

Her voice was calm. 'There was something wrong with Andy's death. Andy had more eagerness for life, more attack, than anyone I have ever known.' Her eyes flicked to the photograph. 'Anyone.'

'It was an accident!'

'I don't think so. There was something wrong.' Mrs Felton straightened her spine. 'I think I might keep bees at Pukekohe. I've always liked the idea of bees. The practice, of course, may be quite different. We shall see.'

Bianca and Gaby's rapport increased, became something more than a way of getting the work done. Gaby had decided that as long as she met up with a few of the guys she used to work with, got this lot out of her hair at night, she could hack it. You can get used to anything. Bianca soon learned that Gaby was what Mother used to call a lovely little worker, a term of approbation she had earned herself in her section-clearing days. They worked well together. Gaby seemed tireless as well as nimble. Her stretch was wide and high, her treatment broad brush; slash and burn, get back to the wood. 'Then we can tart it up, fling the paint around.'

Bianca took over the woodwork, got into the detail. Sugar soap no longer held fears. She was meticulous with the window frames. The wide kauri skirting boards came up well.

'Yeah,' said Gaby realigning her pot of stripper on the top rung of the ladder. 'Comes up a treat, like I said. But why do it now? Let's get shot of the stripping first.'

'No,' said Bianca.

Let her rip. Go with the flow. As long as she keeps at it. Bianca was earning her keep and once Roof got back she and he could steam ahead. After work, weekends, you wouldn't see them for dust. It'd be a pain having the old bat living with them but it should work out okay. A temporary nuisance but once they got the title all would be well. Gaby had every confidence.

As did Bianca. Blessed with equal strength of purpose, Bianca also had no qualms. The essential was to get the title.

They worked on, occasionally fencing around each other, learning how and when incipient battles should be avoided, which ones fought to a standstill and when to retrench. Their skills were complementary, they were united in work for the common cause of their two opposing ends.

Their dissimilar views of ultimate ownership enhanced their enthusiasm in the shared project. They were grateful to each other for their efforts; not overtly, but in their hearts each of them appreciated the other's disinterested acceptance of her role in the fitness of things.

They appreciated each other. They shared what each regarded as a unilateral interest. Admiration was not far away, though Gaby's was tempered by Bianca's implacable stubbornness and occasional loss of a word. She would go silent, you could see her mind groping before coming out with the wrong one. Telephone, say, for toaster; lamppost for lavender. Gran in Matamata did the same thing. Nuts really.

But Bianca was okay. They got on. 'Gee, you never miss a trick, Bee. Talk about observant. And sharp. I'd hate to be stuck in a stalled lift with you.'

Bianca sat back on her heels to stare up the ladder. 'Why? What were you planning to do in the lift?'

Gaby laughed, the ladder rocked slightly. 'There you go again. Sharp as a tack.'

Bianca's stubbornness could be fun to watch too. Especially her reaction to any suggestion of Rosa's. The more simple the proposal, the quicker Bianca's refusal to comply. Resistance was all. Rosa's incompetent parking this morning, for instance. 'Sorry, dear. I'm too near the bush. Don't get out,

I'll back.' In a flash Bianca flung herself out the door into the arms of an overgrown teucrium, found herself unable to open the door wider, pushed harder, burst through, only to be ensnared once more. Rosa got the hedge clippers.

Rosa at lunchtime, dispensing sandwiches and comfort. 'Here's a nice flat place, dear.' Bianca refusing, standing, willing another flat space to appear. She would choose her own flat places. She would be independent in thought and deed. She shared with Mrs Felton, whom Gaby had never met but knew from Bianca was a terrible old woman, terrible, a preference for her own decisions. It was just the scale which differed.

Bianca needed handling. She reminded Gaby of Dad in Matamata. Like Mum said, it was simple. Just a matter of personnel management and keeping the desired end in sight. *The politics of the harem*, she'd read somewhere. Well, go for it. Mug if you don't. All would be well.

The camaraderie which existed between Gaby and Bianca heightened. Rosa's demeaning sense of exclusion from this strange partnership increased.

The dump was her province and seemed likely to remain so. But Henry would soon be home, Henry and Rufus.

Yes.

And Henry and Bianca

Oh dear . . . Oh dear oh dear oh dear.

And how did you and Henry get yourselves into this mess in the first place.

Because of you. This was your idea. Remember.

Martin's condition was worsening by the day and Rosa was in need of rational discourse. 'I'm going to see Martin,' she explained at the back door. 'There's plenty of food in the fridge.'

'Forget it,' said Gaby. 'There's a shop round the corner from Webster Street.'

'Oh goody.' Bianca lifted a hand, added a cryptic 'heigh-ho' and returned to the *Herald*.

Meadowbank was bustling as Rosa drove through and Remuera more so; more trees, more shops, more people, more money. Remuera, it would be fair to say, was basking in autumnal sunshine. Long-legged young women were leaping in and out of large cars, their straight hair flying, their voices high as they herded well-padded young over crossings. One crashed on his behind as the lights changed; his calm expression remained, he was used to it. He was hauled to his feet by his mother. She gave the careful lady driver a smile, half rueful, half 'don't run over us, but I know you won't because old women care'. Old women are not irrelevant. They have their place and like to be useful.

Rosa snarled at the departing backs and swept onwards to the bridge.

A woolly-hatted woman at the next stop adjusted her shopping bag, leaned towards the decrepit old man on the bench beside her to chat as the torn clouds streamed above and the bus was late yet again. He nodded, sat a little sideways and crossed his legs. His mind was on something else.

Martin had given up on his TV. He might as well watch washing slapping about in a laundrette for all the pleasure he got from it. It still loomed, however. Large, vacant as an empty oven, it continued to make a statement of some sort; unused, unwanted, it hung on in there.

He had transferred his allegiance to the radio, was better informed and saved bits and pieces to tell Rosa. A young man had been granted the Delphic award for Pervasive Entrepreneurial and Promotional Ethos. He had been prepared to go that extra mile for Customer Focus.

And there was a good one yesterday. *Top-gallant delight.* Had she heard the phrase? No, he hadn't either. 'Top-gallant delight,' he murmured.

He had been told to give up smoking. Sunnydale couldn't take the responsibility any more. He was killing himself, they said. 'I know that, I told them, and it suits me fine. "But you must think of the other inhabitants," they said. I said why? I told them they needed more customer focus. They didn't like that. They came clean then. I'm a fire risk, they say. So it's very new, you see, this nicotine withdrawal, only a few days and I don't mind telling you it's hell. Let's have a whisky. The bottle's in the cupboard.'

Rosa sat relaxed and dreaming, wondering if she had an empty stomach and, if so, what a good idea. Something was undoubtedly hitting the spot.

A dog barked, one clear yap, then silence.

'How's the cough?'

'Fine.'

Liar. 'Do men have to learn how to spit?' she asked.

'I can't remember.'

'So forceful. Accurate. They must practise as boys.'

He shook his head. 'My friend—Signor Monti in Como always called us that.'

'Tell me about Italy.'

He coughed, and kept on coughing.

'What do you want to know?' he gasped eventually.

'Everything.'

He was breathless, wary, fighting for breath. She brought him water, helped him drink it, sat silent till he recovered.

'Henry's never talked about it. Hardly at all. You know how sometimes when you've done something and it's over you can't be bothered discussing it. Henry's always been like that. If it's over, it's gone. Done. Boring. Rufus is the same. It was like getting blood from a stone finding out, even at playcentre. What he'd been doing. Who his friends were. If you asked him—' her voice dropped, filled with gloom, '"I just played, and played, and played." He's still the same. Don't ask. It's past, over. Like Henry.'

Martin could feel his heart racing. Rosa was not helping either his physical or mental condition. He would have to get on to Henry when he got home. It was a good time to be in Milan; he'd like to hear about it himself. The *lira* half what it had been in '91; about a thousand to the dollar instead of six hundred. Make the sums on the factory floor easier too. Just cut out the noughts.

Remember, Rosa knows nothing. Nothing. All you've got to do is keep off people. But why has she never talked about Milan? Presumably because Henry won't. She'll chat about Paris, the things she wants to see. The bridges, the boulevards she could see herself striding along. The Louvre was overpowering, Henry said. Henry said that snails taste of garlic and nothing else, that she would like the Pompidou, that some people thought it was looking a bit grotty already but that he didn't agree. That he had had little time, there or anywhere. They'd have all the time in the world when they went together.

Had she never wondered about the veto on Milan? Martin looked at her round face, her uncompromising haircut. No, she hadn't.

'And what about Rufus?' he asked. 'How did Rufus get on in Prato?'

She didn't know.

Martin saw Henry and himself returning from Prato in the mid-'70s. They were pleased with themselves, they had done well, extremely well. Henry was expansive, full of praise for Martin's expertise with the language, his quick-witted attack which had been invaluable. Enrico Baronti had been running for cover. They must celebrate, make sure Martin came on every trip.

Martin shook his head. 'No.'

'Whyever not?'

'It's an unnecessary expense now your Italian's adequate. I'd be more use at home.'

A dark-haired woman in black, chic as the early photographs of the Duchess of Windsor and as severe, rose from her chair in the foyer. 'Henry,' she said, 'I must speak with you.'

Martin moved quickly to the tiny lift. '*Piccolo, piccolo,*' gestured the large man beside him. '*Sì sì.*'

That woman and Henry are lovers. That claiming hand, that urgency, every movement of her body. Henry's start, the quick upfling of palms. Five words were enough.

'That woman yesterday . . .' said Henry at breakfast next morning.

Martin lifted his cup for more coffee, '*Grazie.*' His eyes watched the baggy waddle of the departing waiter. 'Don't bother,' he said.

'Was it so obvious?'

'Yes.'

'I'd be glad if you didn't . . . You won't, of course, but . . .'

'No.' Not for your sake. Don't think that for a minute. For Rosa. 'How long has it been going on?' he asked.

'I don't think there's any point in your knowing that.'

'No?' Martin stood up. 'Excuse me,' he said. 'Shit time.'

He had glimpsed Carla throughout the years, had met her occasionally. He did not warm to her. Their acquaintance did not prosper.

'Why do you suddenly want to know about Milan?' he asked.

'Because we'll be going soon. Once Rufus has settled in, when Henry feels completely confident about leaving him in charge we'll be off. We always planned to go as soon as Henry retires.'

He told her what little he knew. He told her about the

elegance and the slums, the grandeur and the kitsch, the pollution and the magnolia and the power of the church. The faith that moves mountains and the corruption in high places. You'll never know it, understand it. You can only love it or hate it.

'It's odd we haven't been before,' she said. 'Ridiculous really. It's easy to park one child. Granny would have been happy. They always got on well, used to make gingerbread men, can you believe. Toffee apples even.' She traced a red stripe on his tartan rug. 'But Henry went off the idea. He said it'd be more fun when he could show me everything, explore together.' She paused. 'You know something? I'd rather have explored by myself. The first time, I mean. I like not having to say things. In galleries when we go, I just want people to shut up. Henry even. I hate it when he talks.'

Martin moved irritably, was furious with her. 'Then why in heaven's name didn't you insist?'

She patted his arm, laughed. 'I can't imagine.' She gave a brisk movement of her shoulders. 'We'll go soon and that'll be great, so tell me more.'

'Let's have another whisky,' he said.

'It's eleven-thirty in the morning.'

'So? There's something else I want to talk about before I run out of puff.'

She came back with their glasses. A deep brown voice sang from the corridor.

Sing lula, lula, lula lula bye bye

Do you want the moon to play with.

Why not. Let us aim high. 'Is yours strong enough?'

'Just.'

'I'll bring a bottle next time.' She lifted her glass. 'Don't die in the night, Martin.'

'That's what I want to talk about.'

She put her glass on the bedside table among the clutter of

what remained of his life: *Best Bets*, crosswords, a *Listener*, tissues, pills and puffers.

'Don't look like that. Lift your glass a sec.' He scrabbled among the papers for a large envelope, waved it in the air.

'Here we are. I've been getting things teed up. I've asked a local padre to do his stuff, no date of course, but that's okay by him. I'll give you this now so you won't have anything to worry about later.' He paused. 'I thought cremation would make more sense. What do you reckon?'

Rosa lifted her game. 'Yes,' she said. 'I'm all for cremation.'

'Good. Good.'

He patted the envelope. 'It's all there, except one thing's a bit of a bind.

'Tell me.'

'The ashes.'

The heart can turn over. 'What do you want done with them?'

'At first I thought just dump them somewhere, but then I thought where? It might be a bit of a bind . . .'

'Don't be ridiculous.'

'They come in a wee box. Quite neat, apparently. I thought you could just tuck it away in the garage somewhere.' He took her hand, gave it back. 'I wouldn't expect you to put it on the duchesse or anything.'

'I haven't got a duchesse,' she wailed.

'The garage then.'

She gave a quick angry toss of her head. 'Right,' she said, smiling into his exhausted eyes. 'Good thinking, Carstairs.'

Rosa, her head backed by elves, sat on the sofa and thought of Martin. Bianca, as usual at this time, was tearing the television apart, tossing and goring the presenters, those idiotic little clouds in the weather map, the advertisements every five minutes. The whole thing made her sick.

Why watch it then? Bianca, the time Rosa had asked her, had replied with insight and a sniff at the garden beyond the window that there was little else to watch. Except the dead sparrow decomposing. Putrefaction, she noticed, had set in, it was rotting before her eyes.

'It is not putrefying.'

'Then what is it doing?'

'Disintegrating. Turning to compost.'

'Nonsense.'

Gaby disappeared each night in her ancient Skoda and returned at varying times, sometimes as they were sitting down to a chop. ('Don't *worry*, no *problem*.') Once in the dead of night she 'knocked something up in the kitchen', something involving pasta and garlic and cheap red wine. The remains were evident next day, the garlic melding with the overnight nicotine. Rosa explained that she was happy for her guests to cook what they liked when they liked, but please would Gaby use the extractor fan. Sure, said Gaby.

Rosa was not one of those people who refused to have smoking in her house. Not for Rosa the long-stemmed cardboard rose and the *No Smoking Please*, and what on earth was the connection? But would Gaby please empty the ashtrays. Sure, said Gaby.

The relationship, as Rosa had come to think of it, between Rufus and Gaby, seemed destined to continue. They had lived together for years and seemed at ease with each other. Toll calls to and fro from Italy had been frequent. Did Rosa like Gaby? Yes. And then again, no. Gaby's good qualities were obvious: loyalty to Rufus, courage in adversity, a lovely little worker and cool as two cucumbers. Yes.

And then again, no.

Bianca, having disposed of two frontpersons with one finger, was also thinking. It was good that her container had been delayed. If there had not been all that muddle and mishandling at the other end it would have arrived long ago and storage in this place costs the earth. The boat had done well to delay. Better still if it became becalmed somewhere en route so the money required for storage on arrival would be negligible. Somewhere safe and possessed of a moderate climate. Excessive heat or humidity or insurrection among locals were undesirable, but so was paying money she could not afford and indeed did not have. She could only hope.

'When do they get back,' she said, 'Henry and Rufus?'

'They'll be in Paris now,' said Rosa. 'In about a week.'

'Good. It will be essential for Rufus to work full time on the house for a while,' explained Bianca.

Pillar-box red lipstick on old lips is a mistake and always has been. 'How on earth can he do that? His weekdays are entirely committed to the warehouse.'

'But what if my things arrive? Henry must be persuaded.'

Stubbornness is a gift as immutable as stupidity. Against which *the gods themselves contend in vain*. Henry had told her.

'Henry will not be persuaded.'

'My things might arrive.'

'Bianca . . .'

Bianca gave a small movement as though adjusting a fall of watered silk about her shoulders. 'We shall see.' Her glance sharpened. 'Why are you drinking whisky?'

Rosa's mouth moved. Was she developing a nervous tic? 'I thought I would like a change. Have you any objections?' She heard herself saying it. Petty, disagreeable, not nice at all.

Bianca ignored her lapse. 'And another thing. I hear that man, what's his name, that friend of yours . . .'

The word 'friend' hung in the air like smoke. It had an aura. It indicated a person who might conceivably be a friend to the misguided but not to those of taste and discernment such as the present speaker.

Auras are hard to fight. They do not come clean.

'Martin Brown,' snapped Rosa.

'Yes.' Bianca was not concerned at her loss of the wretched man's name. The trick is not to fuss, not to snap your fingers in the air mouthing away about things being on the tip of your tongue, how you almost had it, how it has gone again. The trick is to pretend you can't be bothered remembering, which was true in this case. A loathsome creature, Bianca had always thought so. 'One of your lame ducks,' she said.

Rosa's hand shook. 'What an appalling thing to say.'

'It's true, isn't it?'

'No, it is not. Martin is my friend and, even if he were not, no one in the world should be called that. Lame duck. The implication is that, that . . .' Rosa stopped. You cannot say to your sister that she is not only smug but has never known a twinge of lameness in her life when she sits before you, down on her uppers if not her beam ends.

Rosa drank whisky, blew her nose and drank again. 'Lame *duck*.'

'Reeks of nicotine too, the last time I met him. I hear he intends to leave you all his money.'

'Who told you!'

'Gabrielle.'

Exclusion from the playground gossip of others tends to make you puerile, the sense that things told in confidence may whirl around and acquire a life of their own is never pleasing. 'Why were you talking about me?'

'We weren't. You just came up. I can't think why you didn't tell me yourself.'

There was a gleam in Bianca's eye. Rosa saw her at Mother's dressing-table long ago, her small teeth closing on Granny's pearls with the quick instinctive bite of a sailor's moll on a proffered doubloon.

She was now licking scarlet lips. 'It's always so interesting,

I think, these deadbeats, recluses, whatever. There was a woman in New York, I saw last week. A bag lady, had all her meals at a soup kitchen or whatever they call them. Begged any remains and left two million dollars. You never know. You can't tell.'

'No.'

Bianca could wait no longer. 'Is it a lot?' she asked.

Rosa, miserable, distracted and enraged Rosa, lifted her head. 'Yes,' she said. 'It is.'

Martin died a few days later. Arrangements were put in train. The plan was implemented.

Bianca came to the funeral. She felt it was the least she could do for the wretched man.

Rosa told Henry of his death at the airport. He was distressed. They clung to each other. Henry wiped his eyes. He was surprised to find it necessary. He liked Martin and had always done so. Honourable, honest as the day, Martin would be missed, but not much by him. And what a life, the man would be glad to go.

A decent man but not memorable, except, of course, for loyalty. A good man he had worked with forever whose inner thoughts were unknown to him and vice versa. But not entirely. He wiped again.

'Great to see you,' said Rufus, trying to trundle the luggage and embrace Gaby at the same time. 'What's up with Dad?'

'The old guy's died,' she said, 'the guy with the cash.'

nine

It was great to see her again. Rufus couldn't keep his hands off her, let alone his eyes. He hadn't realised, not for a moment had he realised, what it would be like. Too long without loving, too fucking long. Never again, that was for sure. They wouldn't make that mistake again. Gaby must come next time. You bet she would. She couldn't wait. You're a natural, he told her, a born trader. She knew she was, she always had been, she came from a long, long line of wheeler-dealers and horse-traders. Milan, she said, passing the salad, would be a breeze and to hell with the dole suspension.

They laughed, they flaunted, their eyes stripteased. They might just as well have operated here and now, thought Henry sourly, have rolled onto the worn carpet and got on with it. Had they no modesty. Had they no reticence. No, they hadn't. Why didn't they just leave the table, donate their share of the welcome-home carrot cake to Bianca and withdraw to eat each other in private. Leave the rest of them in what he supposed you could call peace.

No, they wouldn't have any more, thanks. Rufus thought he would unpack. 'Coming Gaby?'

'*Honestly*,' said Bianca.

'Honestly what?' he snapped.

'You know.'

Rufus and Gaby lay side by side on the single bed. They talked briefly before love and more later. There was much to hear and tell, to discuss between partners.

Rufus moved a cramped arm. 'You know that weird thing I was telling you about Dad and the Grisoni guy?' She nodded. 'Well, wipe that. I'll start from the beginning. You should've seen him, seen his face. You know when they say "he went green". Fact, absolute fact, I'm here to tell you. I thought he was going to pass out. There we all were in this poncey place and the atmosphere was charged, electric. I mean it. I've never felt anything like it in my life. It was . . .'

'But what did he say, the guy?'

'He told his nephew that Dad had known his mother.'

'So what?'

'But Jesus, you should've seen them. Those guys had him licked, they had him on the ropes . . . It gave me the creeps almost.'

She is now sitting cross-legged by my head. I move my hand, she moves it back. Gaby is a one thing at a time girl. 'Tell me more,' she says.

So I tell her again about Grisoni in the train. I tell her about Grisoni junior. I tell her he's a good-looking guy in a funny sort of way. Dark, intense. I tell her he has a mobile face. I demonstrate. On and on I go, and she listens and she thinks and finally she says, 'I wasn't there. I didn't see any of it, the train, the restaurant, any of these nuances you're on about. *How* were they so real, so threatening? How did you know something was going on, what made it so fucking obvious?'

'Like I said. Dad. You know me, I never notice anything. Not things like, are people well or not. Not what colour they've gone. Normally you'd have to be lying there in a pool of blood, and even then you'd be lucky.'

She's still thinking. Thinking hard. Nutting it out. 'It's obviously one of two things,' she says, stretching; the side effect is her boobs look better than ever.

'Gaby,' I say.

'Mnn? Well, remember where we've got to after.'

'Sure, people can be half dead and I don't notice,' I say later, 'but I do know about power games. I've seen enough, made enough deals. I reckon I could watch a deal in a foreign language and I'd know which guy was winning and which was down the tube. And this time,' I say, kissing her navel, 'it was Dad.'

She moves away. Sits up. 'It's either sex or money,' she says. 'And I'll shoot for sex.'

'Naaah.'

She is serious. 'When Grisoni said Signor Felton "knew" your mother, was it like, you know, biblical?

'Oh come on,' she says at my blank face, 'all that *and he did lie with the woman and he did know her* . . . I bet that's what Grisoni was hinting at. Sex.'

'I don't know.'

'I would've. Can't you even remember which was the most important bit?'

'Oh sure, but it was all . . .' I think hard, see their faces, the spilled brandy. 'The most important bit was where Giacomo said, "That one?"'

'"That Felton?"'

'Yeah.'

'I reckon,' says Gaby, 'that your father had an affair with Giacomo Grisoni's mother.'

I feel rather odd. Not only because the thought of Dad doing it at all is gross, but a mistress, if you see what I mean. How did he find this woman, how did he start, where did they go? And what about Mum? Mum loves him, loves him more than she loves me. It doesn't worry me, never has, why should it. But an affair . . . Dad?

Gaby has grabbed a used envelope and a biro from the floor and is doing sums. 'Are you thirty-five or thirty-six?'

'Thirty-five. That's what he asked. Marco Grisoni, in the train.'

She puts down the biro and nods her head slowly, rocks backward and forward on her neat little bum.

'Get it?' she says.

Henry peered over half-moon glasses at breasts sagging beneath pink knitted cotton. Faded pubic hair was visible below. 'That garment's indecent,' he said.

Rosa was unperturbed. 'No longer a pretty sight? Basically,' she said, climbing into bed, 'I'm a redhead. Or was.' She gave him a quick peck on the forehead and handed him a letter. 'Nice to have you home.'

He flapped the thing away. 'Why now? I'm dead with jet lag, Bianca's on top form,' his head tossed backwards, 'that lot's hot as monkeys. Why now, for God's sake?'

She pulled the duvet to her pale face. 'It's from Martin. He asked me to give it to you. Good night, dear,' she said reaching for the bedside light switch. She sighed, rolled over, remembered Mrs Felton scrubbing Jerusalem artichokes long ago. She had turned, given Rosa the sweet smile which had skipped a generation. 'Have I told you about the first night of our honeymoon?'

Mr and Mrs Felton had been married in Palmerston North. After the reception at the Grand Hotel they had caught the Limited to Auckland, had been shown into the tiny sleeping apartment with its stiff sheets and let-down handbasin. They had edged around each other, smiled, and undressed with decorum. Teeth had been cleaned. Mr Felton bent to kiss her in the bottom bunk. 'I won't bother you tonight, my dear,' he said and climbed the ladder to the top bunk. She lay silent, watching his striped pyjama trousers disappear.

In the morning there was only one *Dominion*. 'Didn't you order one for me?' she asked.

'Why would you want a newspaper?'

She knew then. Knew it was a disaster. It was terrible.

Henry gave a perfunctory pat of the duvet in the general direction of his wife's behind and opened the letter.

> *Dear Henry,*
>
> *They tell me I have pneumonia. This is an odd letter to write. I'm not good at moral decisions, and putting things in writing is never a good idea. But does Rosa know about Milan? The way she looks, the things she asks about.*

The writing became smaller, less precise.

> *I thought I ought to . . . God, I don't know. Come and I'll tell you.*
>
> *Martin*

Henry lay still, stretched his legs. They were aching as they sometimes did after flying. The bed was too small, they should have a bigger one. People have enormous beds now. You have a single and then you have a double and then you die as Martin had died, except his was single. A puriri branch was banging against the roof again. He should cut it off. He would get a man. Eventually. There was a window banging as well. He slid out of bed clutching the letter.

Rosa snapped on her light. 'Where are you going?'

'There's a window banging.'

'The last time it did that was in the *Wahine* storm. The window blew out, there was an awful mess. You were in Milan.' She tugged at the duvet. 'This thing walks,' she said and snuggled down again.

He walked past the now silent lovers and Bianca, who was snoring softly. The gentle nasal exhalations of the sound sleeper followed him down the narrow hall to the kitchen. Moonlight flooded in the wide windows, glinted blue and icy on stainless steel benches. His feet were cold. Rosa was awake—innocent and unsuspecting as a child, she might come padding out to help. He wouldn't turn on the light, couldn't, she would spot the letter immediately. He opened the back door, returned for matches and headed across the porch to the laundry door, removed the key, locked the door from the inside and switched on the light to coconut matting, the washing machine and deep, wide tubs. He held the letter by one corner, set light to it and watched it flame and blacken, then swirled the ashes down the plughole, careful and meticulous as a murderer with bloodstains, rerinsing and swilling till no trace remained.

Weak with relief, he leaned against the locked door. Nothing, ever, in his whole life had given him the security of that gimcrack lock and long-handled key. He stared around the space, sniffed the scent of washing powders, admired bottles, jars, free samples which had never been used. The bench was piled high with travellers' clothes and unironed washing.

Someone, Gaby presumably, had left a half-empty packet of cigarettes on the shelf beside a local builder's calendar labelled *Easy to See*. Above the inch-high numerals a large coloured photograph showed a small resolute child in a yellow safety helmet clutching a bricklayer's trowel and attempting to complete a half-finished wall. *A brickie's nightmare*, said the caption. Men would understand. Real men, do-it-yourselfers with expertise. Henry took a cigarette, lit up and dragged deep. It tasted of dry hay but the gesture seemed appropriate. If no one can see you can do what you like.

*

'Where on earth have you been?' said Rosa.

'Nowhere much.'

'Whose cigarette did you bludge?'

He was about to tell her about the packet in the laundry, how they must be Gaby's, how Bianca would never have been so careless, how . . .

'I don't know,' he said.

'That window's still banging.'

'Jet lag,' he mumbled and blundered out again to the hall. Jet lag, vitamins, nets closing.

She was waiting for him on his return. 'What did Martin's letter say?'

'I think he knew he was dying.'

She made an odd sound somewhere between a gasp and a sniff. 'Yes, but what did he say?'

'For God's sake, Rosa. The morning, I'll show you in the morning . . .'

No I won't. The letter no longer exists. 'I'll tell you about it in the morning,' he said. And where is the letter she would ask? Disappeared. Disappeared where? Down the plughole. Oh Christ.

The rounded curve of her back huffed at him. 'All right. All right.'

When Rufus was about twelve they had cleaned out the back shed, a process Rufus, his eye peeled for loot, had enjoyed. The local tip had been closed. They had driven around Meadowbank attempting to dump half a sack of solid cement. It had been, they told Rosa later, like attempting to dispose of a body. You wouldn't believe how difficult it is to get rid of something you don't want found.

'When are we going to Milan?' she murmured and slept.

Henry did not sleep.

Of all the idiotic things for a man to do. To ask a wife to hand a letter to her husband which dropped mysterious unspecified hints about a place unknown to her. A place her husband went to alone and had done year after year after year.

The danger had not been in the delivery. Rosa, his love who could deliver, had done so without question.

But what was Henry meant to do with these words from the grave afterwards. Rosa, by her very nature, her affection for the man, would want to know his final message to his lifelong friend.

What was he meant to do with the bloody thing?

His irritation did not last. As he knew, he was blessed or cursed with the ability to see the other side. He had never known whether this was tolerance and thus a good thing, or detachment, which was more suspect. Even with Bianca he preferred to move away, to achieve absence or, failing that, evasion. You have to choose the weapons to suit your goddamn psyche.

And Martin, like so many well-meaning instigators of disaster, would have acted from the highest possible motives; loyalty to Henry and, as he had made clear, to Rosa. They had been good friends. She would grieve for the man.

Presumably, he thought, tossing and turning and tossing again, you remember the dead you have either hated or loved. He was a bad hater, but love had worked for Carla and Andy. The rest, by and large, just shuffled off, removed themselves, ceased to be present.

He had been shocked by Rosa's news at the airport; now all that remained was a vague sense of gratitude tinged with irritation for a man who had served him well in the past, if not now. 'Pneumonia, the old man's friend,' the doctor who attended Mr Felton had said. Something to look forward to.

Henry stirred, put his hand on Rosa's sleeping back. Tonight had not been a good start. He would do better in the morning. No, he wouldn't. The letter would loom. And Bianca. And Rufus. And Gaby.

Oh flaming hell. He flung off the duvet and stumbled down the hall to the lavatory.

There is no point in going for a piss in the middle of night unless it is essential, so why do it. There had been a song when Rufus was a child. A comic song about a dustman, a cockney voice drawling, *When y'get my age, it helps to pass the time.* He trickled, spurted, retrickled and trickled again.

He leaned against the wall, gave a despairing snigger. Now he could go back to bed and worry about Rufus and Gaby.

Gaby was a loose cannon, an unknown quotient, a cipher. Henry rubbed his aching shins. He must stop this jargon tossed off by Rufus. How splendid, how wise to be lying awake at dawn making meaningful resolutions about the purity of the language used in tearing what remained of his mind to pieces. Carla had called such sleepless nights *nuits blanches*. He tried again. Cannon was all right, but not loose. Gaby could go off, she could do a grey deal of damage but, like the guns for the defence of Singapore, she faced in one direction only. In Gaby's case, the direction which served her own interests and those of her partner. There would be no change of direction in Gaby's fire.

His mind churned back to Milan, to Rufus.

They had left Milan the day after the meeting with Grisoni. Rufus had made no enquiries, had not raised the topic either during their days in Paris or their journey home. He had, however, seemed preoccupied; not during business meetings, discussions or demonstrations, but during their free time together he had said little, he had not yarned with strangers. Rufus, Henry knew from past years, had something on his mind. Something other than the world at his fingertips—the air hostess at his elbow, his tiny packet of peanuts—was absorbing his thoughts.

Henry knew he should tackle the subject. He tried several

times. He tried at meal times. No, he didn't want his sesame seed roll. Certainly Rufus could have it, and by the way . . . He tried as the green line on the TV screen clocked up seven thousand flight miles and again at nine thousand. He gave up. There are some things beyond the range of words.

As zero five double zero showed on the bedside clock Henry faced facts. He was entirely dependent on Rufus and Gaby's goodwill or, rather, her reaction to his description of the Grisoni meeting. The thought did not cheer him. Nor the sounds of stirring in the room next door. They were talking again. They planned, he remembered, to go straight to the Webster Street house, get a full day's work in seeing it was Sunday. The calendar numerals would be red. People would be buying at the flower stalls of Cimitero Monumentale. Henry closed his eyes and slept.

'Fantastic,' said Rufus, springing about the bare rooms on the balls of his feet. 'Fantastic! You guys have done so much! Who did what?'

Bianca told him. She was happy to do so, she told him how she was an expert on sugar soap now, how it was a joy to watch beautiful wood come up and that she had really enjoyed stripping the scrim though it was an appallingly messy business. My overalls, you wouldn't believe, *and* my hair tied up. But it's wonderful when you see the result. She was quite sorry there were only two small bedrooms to strip, the rest of the house was already gibbed, as he would remember.

Rufus glanced at Gaby. She was at her best when ready for action. She wore black tights, a black long-sleeved T-shirt, and a paint-scarred baseball cap with a purple button. Great body. Tall and skinny, fantastic boobs. Fantastic everything—why didn't Bianca go away, drop dead, bugger off and leave them alone. And Mum would be here in a minute lugging lunch and looking for flat places. Gaby pulled on one of his old shirts spattered with undercoat and looked better than ever. Skinny women do in oversized shirts.

'Who did the high bits?'

Gaby dropped one side of her mouth, gave an exaggerated wink behind Bianca's back and tapped her chest.

'I've just lost a hard-boiled egg,' said Rosa in passing.

'And what did Mum do?'

'The dump,' said Gaby.

'She likes the dump,' said Bianca.

A doorbell rang. Bianca opened it to reveal a man and a woman standing side by side on the verandah. They resembled each other. Same height, same short dark hair, same friendly smiles above matching grey and blue tracksuits. Their expressions, their obvious desire to be made welcome, to please, reminded Bianca of something. Of course, those two on the news, nodding and smiling and bobbing their haircuts at each other. Bianca closed the door slightly. 'No thank you,' she said, her voice firm.

'Did you think we were Bible-bangers?' laughed the man.

'Don't mind him,' said the woman fondly. She produced a business card, gave it to Bianca and smiled over her shoulder at Gaby.

'Phil and Bettina,' she said, 'Clarion Real Estate.'

They were partners, she explained, very keen, go ahead, pro-active but never intrusive, don't get her wrong. They had a special passion and expertise for old houses, especially those in good condition.

'We were just out for a run, lucky we'd just started,' she laughed, 'but actually we live just up the road and we couldn't resist whizzing in for a sec to say if you're ever in the slightest interested in materialising your assets on this highly desirable—or it will be, won't it, Phil? It won't look like this much longer, that's for sure. I mean it was sad with the old lady, anyone could see that, but on the other hand an eyesore like this, well, it drags down the whole street. Sticks out like a sore thumb, doesn't it, Phil? There've been complaints, talk of getting the council on to it, it's been that bad, so really the whole thing's a mercy.'

Phil continued without pause. Yeah, he said. He and Bettina just thought they'd slip in and say hi. They didn't want to be pushy, hell no, but just remember—if you want to realise, capitalise, whatever, we're here. Johnny on the spot, so to speak. Know the locality like the back of our hands. Really taking off, this area, all the up-market gentrification going on, good schools, easy access to town.

Bianca was still at the door. 'Oh no, we're not interested in selling, thank you.' She handed the card back. Thank you,' she said again and moved to shut the door.

Gaby put out a long arm and held it wide. 'Why don't you guys come in and have a look around, see what we've been doing while this slob's,' she gave Rufus's buttock an amiable slap, 'been in Milan.'

'*Milan*,' squeaked Bettina.

Gaby pocketed the business card. *Clarion Real Estate—Action's our attraction. Phil Sharp. Bettina Rogers.* 'Come in,' she said, 'Have a good look round. Watch your feet.'

Progress on the house continued through the winter. Rufus, Gaby and Bianca reached the stage that, with luck, comes after chaos, upheaval and change. The stage when they could nod slowly at each other, their faces serious and tinged with something like surprise as they began to think that maybe they were getting there. Sometimes they said it. Bianca said it and was snapped at by Gaby for being premature. Rosa said it and was snapped at by Rufus. Henry told her a mother's place is in the wrong. He distanced himself as far as possible from Webster Street. He was paying for it and wanted nothing more to do with it. His main hope was that Rufus would be so engaged at the office and working himself blind at Webster Street that he would forget about Grisoni. Stranger things had happened.

As Bianca had told them several times, the days were drawing out. Not like Hampshire, of course, those long twilights, the croquet, the lazy summer evenings heavy with the scent of cherry pie. And the light, ah the light. The softness, the mellowness, the absence of glare.

The longer evenings in Meadowbank, however inadequate, were welcome to her. They meant Rufus and Gaby could work on while she came home with Rosa. Enough was enough. She looked forward to the long soak in the bath while Rosa organised the meal and she was, she explained to Henry's wooden stare, developing quite a taste for gin and water. What on earth would they say in Hampshire. No one drank spirits at home now. Well, hardly.

Rufus and Gaby came back at all hours. Sometimes Gaby did not come back at all. Rosa made no enquiries, offered to leave something to heat up and left it at that.

Rufus took her hand one such night, sat down on the ancient pouffe before her and smiled his smile. 'It's time we had a good talk, Mum,' he said. 'While I've got you alone.'

She smiled back, peaceful and friendly as she remembered them, herself and Rufus and Henry.

Rufus said how much he and Gaby appreciated what she and Henry were doing for them.

'Good,' said Rosa, 'I'm glad to hear it.'

'Yeah, well. But the thing is . . .' The thing was apparently what Gaby called Rosa's intensive care, ha ha. Her continuing never-ending concern for them both was getting to them. Gaby was not used to it, she'd been a free agent for years, they both had, what he meant was . . . Well, Gaby had said just the other day, she had asked, Why doesn't your mother get a life?

Rosa spoke calmly. 'If Gaby doesn't like it, she can leave. Gaby is free to depart any time she wants to. My life is here, in this house.'

Rufus's head jerked upwards. 'Then I'll go.'

Rosa met his eyes. The adrenalin of rage, outrage, frustration, was both liberating and absurd. 'Do that,' she snapped. 'Your father and I have managed quite happily without sight or sound of you for many years. Just as well in the circumstances.'

Rufus, after a quick glance at her flushed face, stared at his boots in silence. Finally he nodded. 'I see that, Mum, and you're a hundred per cent correct. This is your house, yours and Dad's. Not ours, no way. We fit in with you. Great, happy to do so, great to be here.'

He sighed, stroked a wandering vein on the back of her hand, released it, watched it slip back to its original lie. 'It's just . . . just if you'd just back off a bit, Mum. Gaby and I feel sort of, you know what I mean, threatened. Particularly Gaby. She's used to her own space, needs time out. She's into meditation and that helps but . . .'

This was too much.

'And what about Bianca?' Rosa cried. 'She seems to get on very well with Bianca.'

'Yeah,' said Rufus. 'But that's a different thing again and I'll tell you why. You know where you are with old Bee. She doesn't give a toss. Where does she sit? Easy—the best chair. Which bedroom does she claim? The one with the best outlook and most sun. Tough, Bee, that's the master one.' He paused, stroked the loose vein again, watched it move. 'You know where you are with people like Bee. Your trouble, Mum, is you try too hard. You know what you should do? Stop pussyfooting around, be more up front. Honest, don't give a stuff, state your aim and get on with on it. The three of us, me, Gaby, Bee, we all know where we're coming from. What we're looking at. Where we're heading.'

'I see,' said Rosa. She lifted her head, took a long, hard look at this gentle smiling creature still holding her hand. She stood up, clutched briefly at the chair back. She had had a thought, a thought so disturbing it weakened her knees. You can be destroyed as well as saved by what you believe in. You can love too well. Shakespeare, she thought with rage. Shakespeare had it first. Mother, dreamily reading 'my favourite poet' while Rosa ran in with the tea. She was gulping now, gasping with rage. Damn the man. Sitting up there. Knowing it all. Damn the man and blast his genius. Oh God, dear God.

'I'm going to see Granny.'

Rufus, unaware of cross-currents, glanced at his watch. 'It's five-thirty. Be rush hour on the motorway.'

'Good!' said Rosa. '*Good.*'

He looked at her, opened his mouth and shut it again. He and Gaby could pick up a takeaway on the way home. It had gone off okay. Cool. Gaby would be pleased. He headed for the Skoda.

Wisdom lies in learning what to overlook. A useful thought. It fits in my normal system, my philosophy, I suppose you could call it. Forgive and forget. Unto seventy times? Nay, I say unto thee unto seventy times seven. But not today. Fat chance. That's a laugh, Jesus. And why am I so cross with Bianca? And what would Bianca want with forgiveness. Bianca has done nothing wrong. Bianca, as Rufus says, is operating in exactly the way she has operated from the moment she heaved herself upright and padded off to knock the world into a suitable shape for treatment.

So why am I driving too fast? Why am I speeding along the motorway in my husband's car which fortunately he did not drive to the office today, passing astonished vans and old men in Hondas? The motorway is alive with Hondas and I pass them all. I am tempted to make rude gestures but restrain myself. I pass another one and realise my eyes are wet which enrages me further.

I have never been envious of Bianca. Bianca the beautiful has always been cherished by me. Many people have been cherished by me. We all have our gifts do we not, Jesus, and mine is to be unselfish and drive people mad. 'Move *over*,' I roar at a truck labelled *Top Dog*. It blasts its horn. I blast mine. For a moment, one appalling, degrading moment, I think, They'll be sorry when I'm dead, and then I think, Will they? And the answer is not many of them. Henry. Henry will.

The reason I have never been envious of Bianca is simple. It is not from virtue.

Envy is the desire for something you would like to own and do not have. The desire for adulation and antiques has passed me by. That's all.

But jealousy—ah, jealousy is different; meaner, leaner and bitter to taste, jealousy centres on what you have and do not want to lose. Like sons. I am jealous of Bianca because my son admires her more than he does me. This is a shameful thought, corrosive, and piercing as a dart with poison. Jealousy is not a vague sullenness like envy. Anything but.

I am not jealous of Gaby. She has engaged my son's admiration and love. His passion for her is as it should be. Leavest thou thy father and thy mother and cleavest thou to whoever. Rufus had little enough familial affection before Gaby appeared and I want every ounce of what is still on offer, which is silly, for we all know, do we not, that love is limitless and self-engendering. It does not come in pots. It is a bottomless cup.

'Move over, you clown.' I shriek at a man on a yellow tractor at Granny's gate. He smiles, waves at me, I scowl at his red-pleated neck.

And why in the name of all that's merciful did I lie about

Martin leaving me money. What did I think I was doing. Rosa, little Rosa, Rosa honest as the day, lying gratuitously. That's the word—gratuitously—lying for free, for no reason, no sense, nothing. Lying as a child might lie, to counteract rejection, to be allowed to play too. Lying for love, and what do you mean by love? What do you know about love? Everything. Nothing. I am going to explode. Mad, quite mad. *Mad, bad and dangerous to know.* Caroline Lamb and Rosalind Felton. What a pair.

Mrs Felton senior waved from the sunporch. She was at leisure. She lay with her feet up on the ancient humpy couch reading *The New Zealand Poultry Farmer*. The previous owner of the cottage, an old man rake-thin and fading fast, had been asleep in the sun the day she had come to view the house. It had seemed to be a good omen; both porch and couch became desirable selling points. She made her offer that day and has never regretted it. You need sun.

She flicked the magazine in greeting. 'I was thinking about capons, lot of money in capons. Bit technical, of course, but . . .' She swung woollen-covered legs to the ground and sat up. 'Why are you here?'

That's a thought. Why am I here? Rosa picked an open book from the floor. *While female and infant capuchins socialise*, she read, *the males are somewhere else.* She sat down. 'No reason,' she said. 'Just one of those mad irrepressible impulses I have now and then.'

Mrs Felton smiled, slipped tiny feet into ancient shoes. 'Ah, one of those.' Her glance sharpened. 'All well at home?'

'Yes. I've just got a touch of the sours.' Rosa put the book on a table, repositioned it carefully, as though it were important, as important as the placement of a garden gnome with a fishing pole by a proud suburban pond. Rufus had loved gnomes.

'With which one?'

'Me.'

Mrs Felton adjusted her cardigan with a quick twitch. 'No point in that.'

'No,' said Rosa, her eyes still on wildlife. There are upstairs bush babies in the highest levels of the rain forest and downstairs bush babies far below. They never interbreed. They have fingernails. Howler monkeys make the largest noise in South America.

'I told the most ridiculous lie the other day,' she said.

'You haven't come thirty miles in the rush hour to tell me that.'

Rosa gave an unattractive damp snort. 'Oh, do stop going on about the rush hour.'

'I haven't started. Tell me the whopper.'

Rosa's face was strained, pulled tight about the mouth. 'I told Gabrielle that Martin Brown had left me a large sum of money.'

Mrs Felton restrained herself. Laughter is not the right medicine for the afflicted, however comic their wounds. 'Why on earth?'

'And she told Bianca. And Bianca asked me if it was true and I said yes.'

'Two whoppers.'

'Exactly. I said it because I knew it would infuriate her, make her jealous. I wanted her to be jealous. Of me, I wanted them both to be jealous of me. You know what I mean . . .'

'No.'

'That makes two of us.'

They sat in silence. A cattle beast lowed. 'Do you know why the sky's blue?' asked Rosa.

'No,' said Mrs Felton again.

'It's one of ten simple scientific facts everyone's meant to know. I saw it somewhere and I don't know. Not that one.'

How peaceful it is here. Grass oozing chlorophyll, cows chewing, clouds scudding. And no people, no people at all. I have backed the wrong horse as regards peace. Granny has been right all along. She has gone where people are not. You don't have to lie and fuss and grizzle. You can go someplace else. Take time out.

'May I stay the night?' she said.

'Certainly, if you like tripe and onions.'

Rosa grinned. 'Not much.'

'There's probably a chop somewhere. We'll feed the hens. And tomorrow you can go home and stop being so—what's that dreadful word they use now—caring.'

'I am caring.'

'Why?'

'Because I am.'

'Hopeless,' sniffed Mrs Felton.

'You're meant to love people.'

'Worse than hopeless.'

Rosa put her hand on Mrs Felton's knee, begging her to retract, to revoke heresy while the flames licked. 'No, Granny. You've got it all wrong.'

Mrs Felton's voice was stern. 'One minute you're telling lies so you can hate and be hated by your nearest and dearest, the next you're telling me I must love everyone. You're not making sense, Rosa.'

Rosa's face was anguished. 'If I'd made sense anywhere else I wouldn't have come,' she cried.

Mrs Felton stood, brushed her skirt with a quick, impatient hand and stared at her daughter-in-law. Goodness is completely natural to this woman. She is unaware that she is in any way unusual. The knowledge has not penetrated.

'Hens,' she said.

*

Mrs Felton's hens were in clover. Like Aztec sacrificial god kings, they were pampered, tempted with delights and cherished until the knife struck. They ranged far and wide, converging across green pastures at meal times like spokes to a hub.

Mrs Felton watched them, encouraged stragglers with a shake of the feed tin. 'Did I ever tell you about Andy?' she said securing the door after the final head count.

Rosa straightened from her inspection of a skittery white leghorn with blood on its head. It must be low in the pecking order. Or high.

'No,' she said.

Mrs Felton's voice was thoughtful. 'I found a magazine under his bed one morning beside a mummified apple core. Very unusual it was too. Fetishes, women's shoes mostly.' She placed a hand on the rough wooden door frame for a moment, her voice lifted. 'Goodnight, girls,' she called and banged the last chaff from the tin.

Rosa swallowed. There is no end to the surprises contained within this woman. Never has been and never will.

'Why are you telling me?' said Rosa.

'I don't know,' said Mrs Felton, staring across paddocks.

'Did you discuss it with Mr Felton?'

The pale eyes snapped. 'Why on earth would I do that?'

They walked in silence to the next gate. The breeze was soughing in the plantation, moving branches from side to side, lifting and lowering against a pale sky.

'What I do wish,' said Mrs Felton finally, 'is that I had the sense to talk to him about it. That is one of the things that worries me. Something like that, something as simple as a difference of that sort.' She turned to Rosa, her face fierce, her fingers gripping the rusting tin. 'That wouldn't have worried him, would it? Couldn't have affected him in some way? Made him desperate?'

'No,' said Rosa, her heart thumping and her voice firm. 'I couldn't have borne that. The waste.'

Parsley and mashed potato dripping butter and freshly picked spinach helped the tripe slip down, although that is one of its least attractive aspects. Give me bones, chew, texture. Slime and slide are not for me.

It is odd my being here at all. As a child I had gone next door and told old Mrs Buxton I had come to eat cake, which at least made sense. I am not sure that driving, through the rush hour, let us not forget, to eat tripe and sleep on a lumpy mattress in an arctic spare bedroom is rational behaviour at my age or indeed any.

Mrs F's revelation of Andy's predilection has not helped. I do not mean to be glib. I came to confide in Mrs F and she has confided back. Which I had not expected. I do not know what to make of either the revelation or the fact that Mrs F should tell it to me, as casually as if it had happened yesterday, as if she had just remembered this bit of chat. I must talk to Henry.

But a trouble shared is not a trouble spared or halved or whatever the received wisdom promises. Quite the reverse. It is a weakness revealed, by me in this case, to a woman without them. The kapok pillow in the spare room will not help either.

We are all on our Pat Malone. My friend Martin knew that and he told me. I should have told God or nobody. God. Hey, God.

And there is something else now. Another thought I do not like the look of. Why did Rufus send me so many pairs of shoes? Three is not many. Three is three. And he has already bought Gaby four pairs. She told me. Four, she said.

The hairs on the back of my neck rise.

'What are you going to do about your whopper?' says

Mrs F, pouring coffee. The telephone rings and I leap to answer it.

It is Henry. When am I coming home?

I am not, not tonight. I will come home in the morning.

'Why on earth?'

I need, I say, time out.

'Don't be idiotic!'

I nearly tell him he can't take a joke. I don't. I realise that Henry is angry. Very angry.

'I have to take the car in tomorrow,' he snaps.

'Oh. What for?'

Bad tempered, can't take a joke and puerile to boot. 'Servicing!' he yells in triumph.

'I'll take it in when I get back.'

More triumph. 'It's due in at 8.30 am.'

Calm, bitchkin, cool. 'Well, it won't be.'

Mrs Felton takes the receiver. 'Henry, do stop nagging,' she says. 'Rosa will be in tomorrow morning. Goodnight,' she says and replaces the receiver.

My calm melts. Mrs F has gone too far.

Henry stared at the receiver in astonishment. He replaced it, noticed how well it slipped into its mount. Yin and yang. *Home is the sailor, home from the sea.* He examined the fit. Someone had designed it, had made drawings, had worked, thought and dreamed this design. Had planned the ergonomic aspect, the aesthetics, the quality of the product. All this effort involving years of work by a team of experts to benefit the consumer, and he had never given it a thought until this moment.

It seemed wrong somehow.

ten

They sat by side by side backed by Geyser Grey walls, their legs extended on unsanded wood. Their hands dipped to fish, to chips, to chips again. There was a good guy around the corner.

Their silence, filled with chewing or otherwise, was contented.

'Finished?' said Rufus eventually.

Gaby nodded, reached for a cigarette. She lit it slowly, stared at the glow.

Rufus stood, jigged about, stretched and jigged again before collapsing. 'Numb bum.'

Gaby exhaled deeply. 'Tell me exactly what that guy in Milan said?'

'Oh Christ, not again.'

'It's important.'

Indolent, graceful as a cat, she changed position to lie beside him, to watch the smoke spiralling. She put her hand on his chest, waited till his covered it.

'You haven't a clue, have you?'

He yawned. 'What about?'

'How important it is.'

'For Mum?'

'For us, dumb fuck.'

He lay silent, closed his eyes. Two jobs per day was getting to him. She would explain eventually. He wouldn't have to ask.

Her voice was soft, soothing as the fingers removing his cigarette. 'You'll burn yourself,' she murmured.

His eyelids were glued together, his mind a blank. 'Nn.' He smelled the acrid stench, heard the small grinding movement of the butt on the old paint lid.

'Did you hear what I said?'

'Yes.'

There was a quick kick at his thigh. 'Don't go to sleep.'

He made a superhuman effort, dragged his mind back. 'Why for us?'

'Because,' she murmured, 'you know something your father would rather you didn't.'

Rufus's eyes snapped open. 'So?'

She is lying back on her elbows, her face amused, almost pitying. 'So,' she says back.

Something is shifting, floorboards, concrete piles, tectonic plates.

I clutch the ankle inside my old Auckland Grammar sock. 'What do you mean?'

'Oh shit, Rufus. Work it out.'

My hand tightens, she kicks it off.

Her voice sharpens. It happens with switched-on women, it's part of the deal and a pain in the butt. 'Why do I always have to think of everything?' she says.

'Okay. Tell me, smart arse.'

She rolls over on her stomach. 'This place is freezing in winter.' She sits up, brushes her front like Bee, but it bounces.

She is right. You can feel the draught through the floorboards. More than a draught, a bloody gale.

'Well, you can't have carpet.' I stroke the wood. 'It's rough now but it will come up, be a feature. Heart kauri, wood like this, it'd be sacrilege. Besides, there's Bee-baby's rugs.'

She hasn't heard a word. 'It will be freezing. Thirty below.'

I watch her like a hawk watches lambs' eyes. Gaby is thinking hard.

'We would be better off to sell it,' she says finally.

I explain as if she's slipped a cog. 'It's not ours to sell. And besides, the whole idea was for them to get shot of Bee.'

'Onto us.'

'Yeah,' I say. 'Onto us. Get it?'

She is getting mad too. 'I'm not going to live with that old bag.'

'I thought you got on okay.'

'Any old bag would be one too many. And stop treating me like I'm brain dead.'

'You act like it.' I put on a sweet sour voice like an old doll in a supermarket nagging the geriatric trundler beside her who's got parsley when she said persimmons. 'Sell the house, dear? How can we, dear, when it isn't ours to sell?'

'It could be,' says Gaby and uncurls herself. I could watch her stand, sit, bend, move forever.

The door bell rings.

'That'll be Phil and Bets,' she says.

Phil and Bets had just popped in for a minute. They weren't going to interrupt, no way. But they just couldn't resist a quick squiz to see how things were going. They couldn't believe how much had been achieved already. Not if you'd told them. They pranced around the house, demonstrating. Hey, Bets. Look at this. Hey, Phil, over here. Not an ounce of undercoat left, would you believe, and wow, look at those skirting boards. They knew, both of them had realised their potential immediately, or rather Phil had, the only time he'd had a glimpse inside. He'd been flogging chicken shit for the Lions, you should have heard the old girl's language. Well, she had a point, Phil could see that, she was knee-deep in shit already like she said. But even then, just from a glimpse beneath the shambles and muck and newspapers for miles, Phil had seen the potential in those boards. Someone had done a wonderful job on them, that was for sure. He dropped on his haunches to stroke, looked up smiling. 'Great job. Who's the expert?'

Gaby's tongue slid from side to side behind her top lip.

'Bee, wasn't it, hon?' said Rufus.

'The English lady?'

'She's not English. She just talks like that.'

'My aunt,' said Rufus. 'She's going to live here.'

So Gaby and Rufus were doing it up for the old lady as well? Bets thought that was amazing. Imagine putting all this work in to a place you weren't going to own outright. Phil had to say straight out, he couldn't put that sort of commitment in to something he wasn't going to own, period. No, Bets didn't reckon she could either.

'It'll be ours eventually,' said Rufus. 'Come and see the gibbing in the back bedroom.'

They were proud of the gibbing. It had been a killer at the end, they'd been up most of the night, those gib boards can weigh a ton.

Bettina said Gaby must be Wonder Woman. Rufus patted Gaby's behind and told Bets she was so right.

'We haven't painted this one yet,' said Gaby. 'Come and see, before and after.'

They walked down the hall talking. Bettina's cellphone rang. She said she was busy right now but she would get back to the caller later. Not a problem.

They left soon afterwards. Bets promised she'd pop in again soon.

Gaby told her to do that.

'Nice guys,' said Rufus.

'Yeah.'

They stood at the door, watched them walk up the street. Bettina waved her cellphone.

A small girl in a pink satin-topped tutu and ballet shoes danced past clutching a balloon.

'Where do y'reckon she's going?'

'God knows,' said Gaby.

She took his arm. They stayed side by side at the open door. There was not much to see, asphalt, a picket fence, a bottlebrush in bloom. But they liked it here.

'What did you mean,' said Rufus carefully, 'when you said we could own this place?'

She took his arm, closed the door. 'Come and I'll tell you.'

'No,' said Rufus, 'no, I will not. What the hell do you think I am?' He was striding around the empty space, springing from the balls of his feet in outrage. Dust stirred beneath his feet, resettled, stirred again. He turned to face her, dropped onto his heels to squat face to face. 'Apart from anything else, it's illegal. Blackmail is, didn't you know?'

Her eyes widened. Beneath the cropped hair they were huge, misunderstood, famished. 'Who's talking about blackmail? I'm suggesting you talk things through. Find out what it's all about, see if you can help your Dad. The poor old guy's obviously fussed about something. He can't sleep. The toilet's going half the night. It can't still be jet lag after all these months. Talk things through. It's the least you can do.'

They were still eyeball to eyeball. 'Okay, so here we go. "Hi, Dad, what's fussing you . . ."'

'Right.'

'Then he says, "Nothing." Then what?'

Gaby dragged a hand through yellow stubble, wrapped her bent skull in both hands. 'God, you're hopeless.'

'We'll have the title eventually.'

She crossed her legs, lit a cigarette with a virulent pink Bic and blew. 'I wouldn't bet on it.'

His eyes stung with smoke. When he opened them she was standing staring out the naked sash windows to the darkening garden. He was on his feet beside her. 'Now listen . . .'

'Listen nothing. Talk about a dysfunctional family. What a shower, what a pack of screwballs! What am I *doing* here!'

'We're a team!' he yelled. 'The two of us.'

Sudden as rain in Auckland, she calmed down, nodded her head in silence, kept on nodding like a dipping duck. At last she raised her head, looked at him for a moment, then smiled into his eyes. 'Okay. So I'll talk to him if you're so shit scared.'

'Why?' he begged. 'What good will it do? We can't kick Bee out, title or no title.'

'Who said anything about kicking her out?'

Gaby stroked the pink lighter, turned it over, stroked again. 'You know something? I wouldn't trust your Auntie Bee with a flat tyre. She's as ruthless as your Dad's gutless. How'd she get him to buy it in the first place? I reckon she's got some sort of lean on the guy.'

She lit a cigarette, sighed through smoke. 'I'd hate to be in her power.'

'You smoke too much.'

She kissed him, her lips warm and smoky. 'Any other complaints?'

The rain began as they were tidying up, fat drops splashing from a dark sky. By the time they reached the Skoda it was torrential, lashed horizontal by the sudden storm.

'You'd better drive,' said Gaby. 'I can't see in this muck.'

The gutters were full, water was swirling across intersections, flash flooding down drives. The wind increased, broke branches, rattled and banged and roared through Meadowbank. The Skoda leaked.

Henry opened the door for them. 'A rough night,' he said.

'Yeah.' Rufus glanced around the dark sitting room. The only light fell from beneath a drunken pleated shade above Henry's chair. 'Where is everyone?'

Henry picked up the paper. 'Bianca is having an Early Night in capitals. Much good may it do her in this racket. And your mother, fortunately, had already decided to stay the night with Granny.'

'Why on earth?'

Gaby dropped her wet parka on the floor and sank onto the sofa.

Henry stared morosely at print. 'Carnage,' he said. 'Chechnya, Rwanda. When's it going to end?'

'I don't know.' Rufus flopped on the sofa beside Gaby. 'Is Granny sick then?'

'No. Your mother said she wanted Time Out. She's also in to capitals tonight.' He flapped pages, folded, soothed, laid them to rest beside his chair. 'The difference being, of course, that Bianca is always in capitals. Everything she says or does or eats or thinks requires them. They are hers, ergo, they cap. I hope to God Rosa's not catching it.'

'Time out? Mum?'

'That's what she said. To give her her due, she was sending it up. Rosa doesn't need cant. She just goes away and has a good sulk, like any other sensible human being. Or cat. Cats are great sulkers, but you can enjoy them.'

Rufus stared at him. Even a non-noticer will notice if the head is spotlit. The old man looked tired, his hair in need of a wash, the lines on his face deepened by shadows. He was banging on, talking crap, shuffling his feet back and forth on the non-existent pile of the carpet. Rufus could not remember Rosa ever having left him alone before, even for a night. It was mad, he had told her, crazy. Shit, he leaves you enough. And here was Henry, bereft, ill at ease already.

As was Rufus.

His father was still talking. 'Have you ever noticed Bianca's unusual emphases? She does it continually, some women do, saves thinking, I suppose. But Bianca's a ripper. She goes for the adverbs. She *thoroughly* enjoyed her lunch with Naomi Fitchett. Why are we told how thorough her enjoyment was? Unlike others' sweaty old enjoyment, Bianca's enjoyment was the dinkum oil—fully paid-up enjoyment while the rest of us slobs have to make do with . . .'

Rufus stopped listening, caught Gaby's eye while Henry rattled on. Her mouth moved, exaggerated, silent and pregnant with meaning. *Now. Tonight.*

Give us a break, he mouthed back. She didn't get it, but his face was enough. She yawned, put a long-fingered hand to her mouth. 'Pardon me,' she said, 'but I'm stuffed. Night.' She put a hand on Rufus's head in blessing and left.

He turned to watch, was rewarded by a wave and a damp smacking kiss in the air. He could see her bony arms clutched around her, her bounding strides along the passage, her unspoken trust.

Henry was lying in his chair with his eyes closed.

'Dad?'

The eyes opened, took a moment to focus. Rufus lit a cigarette, offered one and was refused. Had Rufus not noticed he was about the only person left in the place not puffing his head off?

'And Mum.'

'As you say.'

'Why hasn't she come home?'

'I told you. Time bloody out.'

'Oh, come on, Dad.' Rufus leaned back. 'The springs in this thing are shot.'

'Very possibly.' Henry heaved himself upright. 'Now if you'll excuse me, I think I'll go to bed.'

Rufus could feel his heart pumping. Adrenalin. Power. Shame.

'Does Mum know Mr Grisoni?'

Henry sat down. 'No.'

Rufus leaned forward to flick ash. Memo: Tell Gaby. Dad didn't ask which Grisoni.

'Why do you ask?'

'I just wondered.'

Henry stretched his legs, examined a polished shoe. 'How could she? She's never been to Italy.'

Rufus's jaw clamped tight. He nodded slowly. 'True,' he said. 'True.' There was a pause, quite a long pause before he looked up smiling, to ask the next idle question. 'What was Grisoni senior on about that night?'

No daggers in that smile. It was comradely, understanding. Henry's heart moved in response. Decent of the boy not to rush him, to give him time, to wait for the right moment to talk man to man.

He was tempted to confide in him. He had never confided in anyone, except Andy. You only need one.

There need be no details, just a sentence would do. I had an affair with his sister-in-law. For years. For years and years and years.

Rufus, perhaps, might understand. Isn't that what happens among comrades, between members of a fraternity. They do not need things spelt out. They know the rules. They tolerate, forgive, but most of all they understand.

But not sons.

The reason I cannot tell you I have betrayed (too strong a word, but then again not) your mother, Rufus, is because she is precious to me, essential. I have always loved her. In a different way from Carla, of course. In my fashion.

And, let us not forget, I never had these qualms of conscience, never felt the need to be absolved when the likelihood of being found out was minimal. When Rosa was innocent and Martin loyal to the end, Henry was carefree. Too happy, happy Henry.

We are all going to pay for our train rides. The presence of the conductor merely confirms this intention.

He had lived a charmed life for thirty years. He would not lose it now, not what remained. He thought of himself snapping down the telephone at Rosa. He wanted her, needed her sitting beside him, her small hand in his.

Rufus's kind eyes were waiting for his.

Henry smiled back. 'It's a long story. How about a whisky?' He stared out the drenched window at the storm still flattening the garden. 'It's a good night for it. We must do something about that branch of the puriri.'

Rufus grinned. 'We?'

'All right. You.'

Henry walked slowly to the kitchen. He had the bones of his skeleton story hanging together, had had since Milan and the long flight home. He had taken them out to check occasionally, had shaken them briefly and put them back in their closet. Bare bones only, but available.

Henry squinted through amber. 'Happy days.'

Rufus raised his glass to the dark window. 'Nothing like a good storm when you're not out in it.'

Henry told his story. He explained that the mutual dislike between himself and Marco Grisoni went back many years.

'Like thirty-five years?'

'Longer,' said Henry.

Grisoni senior was ruthless, manipulative and had the business ethics of an alley cat. He was also abusive and a bully. The woman he mentioned, Henry had indeed known her . . .

'Carla Grisoni?'

'. . . Yes.' He had had occasion to rescue her, literally, once many years ago, at a restaurant. Grisoni had been drunk, the other guests had left in disgust, Grisoni was storming, out of his mind, insisting she eat his zabaglione. She didn't want it, was in tears, begging for mercy, then Grisoni suddenly lurched off to the mens and he and Signora Grisoni had slipped away. The man had never forgiven him.

Henry gave Bianca's long, pained sigh. '"Terrible man. Terrible."'

Rufus took a pull on his whisky. 'Doesn't look the sort of guy to fuss about a pudding.'

'No.'

'Why did Giacomo say, "That one?"?'

'Obviously his uncle had told him of the incident. All those years ago. Extraordinary.'

Rufus lit a cigarette, watched the smoke. 'Festered, do you reckon? The insult?'

Henry looked up sharply. Rufus smiled back. 'So you didn't have an affair with the lady?' he said gently. 'Nothing of that nature.'

'Good God, no.'

'Mmm. Mum'll be interested. Be something new to tell her. She's always on to me about Italy. Who do we see, who do we meet in Milan? Human interest is meat and potatoes to Mum. It's a drag punting up stuff to keep her happy. Look, Mum, I say, give us a break. It's over. It's happened. I've forgotten.'

'No,' said Henry. 'There's no point in telling your mother.'

Rufus smiled, patted the bony knee beneath the tweed. He sang the weepie slowly.

'*Hush, not a word to Mary,*
She might not understand.'

Henry stared at him without emotion. He had none. It had disappeared, gone somewhere else. Left him dry as a burnt sack. Did he know what he was doing to him, this man, this buffoon in front of him.

Henry stood up, stumbled slightly, righted himself. 'Very well,' he said and headed for the door. He turned around, hesitated. Where was he going? There was nowhere to go. He turned, gripped the architrave.

'Rufus,' he said to this stranger. 'I think I should remind you that you are entirely dependent on my goodwill and your mother's. We own the house you and Gaby intend to live in.' He paused, a muscle twitched. 'With Bianca.'

'I know that, Dad. I've told you how grateful I am, we are . . .'

'We?' said Henry.

Rufus nodded. 'But the thing is, Dad. Come back and I'll tell you.' Rufus leaned forward, put his cards on the table. 'I don't trust Bianca. That's something you have to hoist in. That's my gut feeling. Nothing to do with Gaby. I like Bianca, don't get me wrong. We both do. But . . .'

Henry knew what he should say. He heard the words forming in his head. He should tell his son that he understood perfectly, that not another word was required, that he realised that Rufus knew the truth and if his father did not hand over the Webster Street title he would explain to his mother that her happy marriage of over thirty years had been a mockery.

He should tell his son to leave the house and not return. He should strip layers of charm from the man and tell him to fuck off. To publish and be damned. There are words to demolish treachery, words waiting for use.

Words he would not use.

A love affair of such length, which had begun while his wife was pregnant, cannot, however deviously, be presented as a casual fling to be expunged by time. Rosa would be the fall guy of a bad joke, her trust confounded, her innocence betrayed. Rosa, the proud loser, would leave him. She would love him, and leave him.

He came back and sat down, picked up his abandoned drink.

'Why do you not trust Bianca?'

'Now don't misunderstand me. Bianca and I get on well. She's been good to me. But she's a total egocentric, know what I mean?'

'Yes,' said Henry.

'I feel, and okay, yeah, Gaby does too, that when she gets all her gear around her she'll want to get shot of us, to expand. There's no room for all her stuff. It looks crowded already. Stuff like that needs space, room to be seen.'

'Rufus, I don't think you understand. Bianca cannot "get shot of you" because she doesn't own the title. And how could I be sure you wouldn't get rid of her?'

'For God's sake, Dad!'

Henry did not look at him. He took a gulp of whisky, held it in his mouth. The sensible thing to do would be to hate, but that had never been an option.

'I'll require confirmation, in writing, from you that you will make no attempt to get rid of Bianca.'

Rufus lifted his empty glass, peered through it. 'If you insist.'

'I do.'

'Okay.'

'And you'll . . . ?'

Henry heaved himself upright. 'Turn the light out when you come,' he said, 'and check the windows. It's getting worse.'

Gaby sat up in the dark. 'Okay?'

Rufus slumped onto the other bed, pulled off his Reeboks and stayed sitting. 'Yeah.' His hands hung low between his knees. 'Jesus wept,' he said and rolled over.

'Come over here.'

'No, I'm buggered.'

She tried again in the morning. Had he or had he not got

the title? What had Henry said? How was she to know what was going on if he wouldn't tell her what the fuck happened. She flung clothes on as though she hated them, strode around the room, waved her arms and snarled.

Rufus let her rip. It was unlike Gaby, cool, laid back Gaby. He continued dressing in silence: suit, tie, all the gears to keep him together, to stop him falling to pieces and hitting the fan.

Finally he rounded on her. He tugged his Italian silk tie donated by Signor Monti throttling tight and told her. He was virtually sure that Henry would give them the title to the house, that he had done as she had suggested and he would do no more. If she wanted details she could ask Henry. 'Ask him,' he yelled and stormed out the door to catch the bus.

He passed Bianca in the hall. She had had a terrible night. Terrible.

Henry also caught an early bus.

Rosa came home to watery sunshine and an empty house. She walked around smiling, plumped a cushion, plucked a dead daisy from a vase. This is what it would be like when they had all gone; old shoe comfort once more with her friend Henry.

No lies, no idiotic behaviour, no jealousy. Normal service would be resumed as soon as possible.

She would ring him. Hullo, love. It's me. Will you pick up the car? Great. See you later.

And today she would catch up on the *Guardian Weekly*s. She would read them as Henry read them. She would start at the beginning and go on to the end. She would no longer snatch and grab headlines, or life, on the run. She was no fool and would cease behaving like one. Time is the art of the Swiss and not only the Swiss. What you do with what you have is up to you.

*

Time passed, they used their days. What else could they do with them. Tensions ranged from Henry's, who was either virtually moribund or irascible, through Gaby's silence and Rufus's preoccupied frown to Bianca's blithe unawareness of anything unusual in the home. She stood and watched rain fall. There had been a lot of rain in Meadowbank, the dead sparrow had either sunk or been buried. She did not bother to inquire which. It had gone, which was an improvement, and soon she would be counting the days, soon her container would arrive. Soon she would be surrounded by her own things in what would shortly be her own house once she had had a word with Henry. She would wait until they had made the move. There was no point in rushing it. Things would fall in to place. Speed bonnie boat.

Rosa also was calm. Her brush with hysteria had passed. She had ceased going to Webster Street. Her dumping skills were no longer required. She would run up some new cushions. She had not yet confessed her lie but she planned to do so and would when the opportunity offered. She could not think how she had got herself in such a state.

Mrs Felton was definitely going into capons, she had been to see a man nearby and had Rosa got over the sours? Good. Good.

But Henry was a concern. He had always been a comparatively silent man and, like his father, prone to sorrow at the state of the world. But he had been amusing, fun to meet and greet, an amiable man to have about the home and seldom bad-tempered. Rosa still felt pleased when she saw him loping up the street from the bus with his longer-legged version of Rufus's prance. Now things were different. His gloom was constant, his parsimony, or rather his concern for money, increased. It was like living with Scrooge McDuck.

At night in bed he was loving and tender. More so, if anything. And unhappy. She had tried to help.

'What's the matter?'

'Nothing.'

'Oh, come on, Henry.'

'We'll need new tyres soon.'

She felt like telling him not to mind, that she would kiss it better. 'Worse things have happened at sea,' she told him.

'The two back ones.'

And he was not sleeping. At night when not holding her close he behaved more like the Ghost Who Walks than a demented duck. It was not funny. It was not funny at all.

Rosa got into the garden and stayed there. Each day was filled with the resurrection of lost treasures and the restoration of mangled remains. The garden centres were in bloom: punnets of pansies for instant glow, groundcover and bright bedders by the mile.

They did the packing themselves and Rufus hired a van.

'*The great day dawned bright and sunny*,' said Rosa. 'Remember Bee? School essays. *What I did in the holidays*.'

Bianca inspected the last of the boiled egg she had requested. She was going to have a Big Day. 'No.' She peered closer and put down her spoon. 'This *egg*,' she said, 'has been *fertilised*.' She moved the plate away with a little shiver of rejection.

Henry laughed. 'Do you the world of good.'

Gaby agreed. A bit of what the rooster did would set Bee up a treat for her big day. She winked at Rufus. He avoided her eye, looked across the familiar room at the new cushions glowing in a corner. They showed up the rest, made them look more faded and beat up than ever.

He found himself on his feet. He just wanted to thank Mum and Dad for all they had done over the past months for them all. He couldn't thank them enough and he'd like to take the chance to say how very much . . .

Henry, his face tundra bleak, stood up and walked from the room.

'No, no, no,' cried Rosa. 'We were happy to, weren't we . . .' She stopped, confused by Henry's departure.

Bianca and Gaby gazed at the speaker. Bianca in surprise, Gaby with something like concern.

The timing of Bianca's boat was perfect. It sailed in to the container wharf a fortnight after the move and her container was transferred to Webster Street with dispatch. Bianca had to admit she was quite impressed.

She was excited as a child at Christmas, joyful and triumphant and determined to unpack each gift herself. No one must help. She stood in the centre of the still-empty sitting room and explained. Certainly Rufus could help with the furniture. She couldn't handle that. She gave a small throaty chuckle. 'But in the meantime—no thank you, Gabrielle, I'd rather do the china cartons myself. It will be lovely to see them all again.'

It was not. It was heartbreaking. Many things were broken. Many, many things. The toll mounted; shards of Derby lay beside broken Worcester, a Meissen parrot had lost its beak, a pug an ear, an early chocolate jug lay in fragments.

Bianca, who minutes before seemed about to hop on one leg from sheer wanton joy, was now beside herself with grief. She knelt beside the wreckage, her normally calm face twisted, her arms wrapped about her head as she rocked backwards and forwards, backwards and forwards, keening with the agony of loss.

Her things, her things, all her pretty things smashed to pieces, broken beyond redemption, lost and gone forever.

Rufus and Gaby stared at her in bewilderment. Rufus dropped on his knees beside her, attempted comfort. Mentioned insurance. Damages.

Bianca scrambled to her feet, tripped, stumbled, straightened herself and came at him, her fingers stiff, her face a mask of hate. 'Insurance!' she screamed. 'What use is *insurance*? They are *gone*. Gone, you fool. Gone.'

Rufus wiped spittle, backed instinctively. 'The container must have been dropped. You can sue.'

His lack of comprehension fuelled her despair. '*Sue*. What's the point of *sueing*.' She became incoherent, flung wrapping material about, wept for her treasures, her vanished trove. She seemed to have none of the blinding rage he would have expected against those responsible for the tragedy, no steely desire for revenge, for recompense to soothe her broken heart. This was true grief, naked and pure and incalculable.

'You can get some of them mended,' said Gaby.

Bianca stared at her in horror and collapsed. She fell in a heap on the bare boards and lay weeping. Gaby dropped on her knees beside her, took the grey head in her arms and stroked it. 'There, there, Bee,' she said. 'There, there.'

Rufus stood silent beside the wreckage, looking at his partner. Her eyes were damp with tears as she bent to comfort, to help the distraught old woman.

'Come on,' she said. 'I'll get you a hottie. Roof and me'll sort this out.' She helped the trembling woman to her feet, guided her to the door. 'Okay?' she said, 'okay?'

She came back to the sitting room, and sank cross-legged beside him. He had finished the unpacking of the damaged carton. It was a sorry sight. Totalled, virtually totalled.

'See what I mean?' she said.

'Poor old girl,' he muttered.

'That's not what I mean.'

Bianca's grief had disturbed him. He was no good at it. He frowned, focused his eyes on hers and waited.

'She's out of her tree,' said Gaby. 'Completely. One hundred per cent, like I said.'

He didn't remember her saying that and said so. Gaby lifted a hand, flicked the charge to the tiled fire surround. 'She's lost it. Completely lost it. Have you ever seen anything like that performance? She needs counselling, professional help. And quickly.'

'She was upset,' he muttered.

'You can say that again.'

They discussed Bianca at some length. Bianca was all right. Bianca was not, Bianca would need watching. Gaby had met hysterics before, some complete flakes, junkies, the lot, but never anything like this.

'Have we got any beer?' she said suddenly.

'A couple of cans. Why?'

'Let's go and see Phil and Bets.' She flung her arms about, demonstrated lack of air.

Bianca was asleep when they left.

'See?' said Gaby.

Rufus shook his head. He didn't see, he didn't see anything.

He had followed Henry after his abrupt departure during his words of thanks, had found him in the office staring vacantly out the window. He had tried to communicate with him, to get things on line. He stood at the door, hating the el cheapo desk, the sleazy chair. So much for fucking style.

'Dad?' he said.

Henry turned. 'I have changed the title to your name as you requested. If you say one word, and I mean just that, of this transaction, I'll change it again.' He smiled. 'To Bianca's name.'

The smile, that loaded smile reminded Rufus of Milan. He saw Marco Grisoni and his father. Saw brains which had turned to brawn.

He told Gaby about the title that night. She was delighted. He left out the smile. The smile had upset him, upset him a lot.

eleven

And then came the good weather, the early summer days with not a hint of humidity when al fresco hits the city and Aucklanders realise yet again they have it made. When the scraping of hulls and painting is finished, the rush to get the boats in the water over and the yachties' winter work done. Now comes the good part. They have earned it and will go for it, weekend after weekend the whole summer long, they promise each other in pubs all over town and glasses and stubbies are lifted and eyes acknowledge and wink back. This is the life. Work's a bitch but there'll be time over. All the time in the world. This is what life in Auckland's all about, they say. Too fucking right. Long summer days when North Shore commuters fall off the bus and down to the beach, in theory if not in fact, to be greeted by wives and lovers and small naked children scurrying to welcome. Gosh/shit, say the women as they slap sunscreen on wriggling brown bodies. Is it that time already?

In these days Bianca recovered her calm, or most of it. No one would ever know or understand her loss. She realised this immediately. Gaby, Rufus, even Rosa seemed to think she was fussed mainly for mercenary reasons. That she was some sort of snivelling miser who had met her comeuppance. They had no concept of her worship of the beauty of craftsmanship, her delight in the authority of each slashing brush stroke on an early blue and white bowl, in the depth, the warmth of old porcelain. How could they understand her sacred reverence for the skills of the unknown artists who had fashioned the fluted shapes, the fenestrations, the purity of line and colour she had owned and lost.

'You're the expert, darling,' Justin had said. 'They're your treasures.' And she was and they had been and were gone.

But Bianca was a strong woman, a woman of courage. She knew that, everyone in Titchfield had known it. No one, they said, no one but you, Bianca, could have nursed Justin for so long. And as lovingly. And she had. She had always treated the moribund husk of her husband with respect, had put his hand out to shake the hands of others, had covered for him, anticipated disasters and laughed off accidents when she could. But not at the end. No one could have at the end.

Bianca pulled herself together. Her loss was hers alone and she would deal with it. She unwrapped the shards Rufus had sorted and rewrapped them in clean white tissue paper from Whitcoulls. She had rejected the sheaths of rainbow colours proffered by Bronwyn. Bianca knew she was Bronwyn, the squitty little cash sale ticket said so. *Whitcoulls*, it said, *Sales person Bronwyn. Always something new.* Bronwyn, a funny little thing but pleasant, advised coloured tissue, but Bianca remained firm. She had been tempted for a moment to tell her why, which was foolish. This loss could be shared with no one. No one would understand. She stood feeling faintly sick, clutching her handbag with both hands in front of the smiling Bronwyn, backed by birthday cards and get well cards and sympathy and bereavement.

Bronwyn was as kind as she looked. 'Are you all right?'

'I . . . Yes, thank you. Yes.'

*

She rewrapped her broken treasures with the calm competence of a nurse laying out a corpse. The spirit had gone, only the broken shells remained. The remains of those beyond repair would be stowed with dignity. Her fingers lingered over special treasures, her eyes noted rare marks but remained dry. There would be no more nonsense, her treasures would be mourned in silence and should have been from the beginning. More were retrievable than she had hoped. She would mend them herself, take a course. The thought appealed, sank in, filled her sad heart. She would find a china-mending expert, apprentice herself, learn the trade secrets and set herself up. She would make money at home and work part time in an antique shop. She saw herself, polite but obviously knowledgable, moving forward to help, brushing aside a velvet curtain to assist, to explain, to share her knowledge. She would be well dressed but not intimidating. It would give her somewhere to wear her clothes. Now she was behind the velvet curtain with the owner, a figure faintly reminiscent of Barry and as amusing, but an older man, dignified and courtly as the experts on *The Antiques Road Show*. They sat side by side with two steaming cups of real coffee surrounded by the backstage clutter of their profession: the reference books, the lists of hallmarks, a Strawberry Gothic hall chair without a leg, an Irish cream jug in need of repair. Why had she not thought of it before? Vistas, whole new vistas could open up, would open up. All was not lost. Good things can and do rise from bad.

She divided the remains into two, those beyond redemption and those to be mended. The redeemable box she hid beneath the bed in her room, the lost treasures she stowed beneath the house when Gaby was out. She unlatched the little door in the foundations at the back, bent double and crept inside dragging the box of shards to lie with concrete piles, cobwebs and a few slaters trundling across baked earth. She sat in Rosa's overalls beside the cardboard carton for a few moments, breathing in the sour smell of concrete and dry clay. There was a spider spinning a web. You don't often see that, any more than you see a hen actually laying an egg. She watched it swing into space, fasten itself, scamper round to swing again. Fascinating, and remember Robert Bruce. Bianca climbed out, feeling at peace and strengthened. She would tackle the next box.

Which was better, infinitely better. Gaby returned to find her crooning the 'Eriskay Love Lilt' among lidded tankards and rat-tailed spoons.

'Hi.'

'Oh, hullo, Gaby.'

Gaby picked up a silver beer mug. 'Nice stuff.'

Bianca smiled at the odd-looking child. The clown-like hair was longer now, sticking out in clumps around the small pale face. 'I think I should tell you, dear,' she murmured, 'your roots are showing.'

Gaby clutched her head in mock horror. 'My Gaad!' She gave the urchin grin of a small boy, pulled out a packet of gum and proffered it. 'I'm trying to cut down.'

'No thank you.'

'I've been thinking. Would you like to borrow the Skoda tomorrow? Give yourself a break. Get out, go for a bit of a run. You've been working your butt off round here.' She looked around the room. 'Looking good though, isn't it?'

There is something hypnotic about chewing jaws. Bianca, touched and surprised, had a thought as she watched them. A thought so good, so strong and enterprising she almost whistled. 'That's very kind of you,' she said, 'I'd like that very much. I'm a very good driver, as you know.' She stood up. 'By the way, have you seen the Yellow Pages anywhere?'

'Down the hall.'

Bianca skipped down the hall, laid the Yellow Pages on the newly wiped bench and turned to Antiques.

The Skoda's gears were interesting but not impossible. Bianca drove through the suburbs smiling. She had her map, her list, her plan. The whole of Auckland was sitting out well to the sun, waiting for her this clear sparkling morning. She could hear her voice. I'm not afraid of hard work, she would say. My nephew and his friend and I have just completely refurbished a derelict house.

Later, when they knew each other better, she would ask her employer, she or he but probably he, to see her things. She could hear his appreciative murmurs, his informed comments. She would own the house by this time and he would call in for a sherry on his way home and they would sit and talk, discuss their day together, the laughs they had had, their customers, the sales made or hoped for. Gin perhaps, when they knew each other well. And champagne to celebrate the partnership.

Her glow abated as the day wore on. Half the people who called themselves Antiques were Collectibles and many were Second-Hand Tat. Colonial were the worst, acres of rose-wreathed chamber pots, a scrubbing board, a flat iron, a mirrored umbrella stand with knobs. And teddy bears. Bears, black, white and khaki, dirty bears and clean, cross-eyed and squinting, everywhere there were bears. She gave one startled glance at an enema can and left.

It was getting hot. Bianca ate a dubious slice of quiche and felt worse. It was not till well after lunch that she came to a real shop, a small and beautiful shop owned by someone who knew what he was doing.

There was even a velvet curtain of the right colour, that faded, muted no-colour Barry had laughingly called Elephant's Breath. Seated behind a flat leather-topped desk in front of it, a plump pussycat of a man was attending to his affairs. He looked up, smiled politely. 'Can I help?'

Bianca sat opposite him on a ballon-backed mahogany dining chair and explained her business. All around her wood gleamed and colours were subtle. She caught her reflection in a pretty little French mirror. She was a collector, she explained, well, in a sense, not so much a collector as one who happened to have . . . she waved a hand, the man put down his Parker and nodded. But unfortunately some of her treasures had recently been broken and she wanted to learn how to repair them and could Mr . . . ?

'Holmes.'

'Thank you, Mr Holmes, could you help?'

Mr Holmes explained that there was a very good woman in Levin.

'*Levin*.'

'Yes. She charges the earth but they all do. Time consuming. Very, she has jars full of spare fingers, rosebuds. It's a life's work.'

'I can't go and live in Levin.'

Mr Holmes, with infinite courtesy, indicated this was not his problem.

Bianca changed tack. She had no hesitation, she was as direct and purposeful as ever. She wished Mr Holmes to know that when and, of course, if, he needed a part-time employee she would be happy to help. She looked around the small, beautifully furnished room, the perfect groupings, the curtain. 'Very happy,' she said.

Mr Holmes picked up his fountain pen once more. It was one of those gold-nibbed mottled ones; new, but pretending to be old. He gazed at it thoughtfully then put it down with a sad little smile.

'How long have you been back in New Zealand, Mrs . . . ?'

'Lefarge. Bianca Lefarge.'

His sorrow appeared to deepen slightly. 'Bianca Lefarge,' he murmured.

'I've been back, good heavens, over six months. More.'

He nodded. 'And may I ask how long you've been away?

Bianca gave a light little laugh of astonishment at her reply. 'Thirty years.'

'About five years longer than I.'

'Ah,' Bianca laughed again. 'I thought so. Your voice.'

Mr Holmes looked more miserable than ever. 'New Zealand, Mrs Lefarge, has changed. Is changing every day.'

'Oh I realise that. All this awful . . .'

'Let me explain. People like ourselves, expatriates who have returned to the land of our fathers are now as outdated, as irrelevant to our country as the returning members of the British Raj were to theirs. Those men and women who spent their working life longing for Home . . .'

'I didn't.'

'I did, but let that pass. I could not employ you, Mrs Lefarge, because I do not make enough money. I make very little money. The days when the emergent wealthy, the young or not so young bought old furniture in New Zealand have gone and very sensibly so. Our light does not suit the past, Mrs Lefarge. It is fierce and strong. Old things, particularly furniture, bleach, fade, fall apart, require cherishing and time and effort, none of which people here are prepared to give to things any longer. If, of course, they could afford them in the first place.'

Mr Holmes's pleasant voice flowed on. 'However beautiful, however treasured, our antiques, Mrs Lefarge, are old hat. Some things fit, of course. Pine, anything which can . . .'

'*Pine.*'

'Pine.' He smiled. 'Our possessions, like ourselves, Mrs Lefarge, are an endangered species.'

The man was mad. Barking mad. 'All my friends . . .' Bianca

paused, distracted, appalled. Friends? What friends? Naomi. Naomi who? Oh please God. 'My nephew,' she cried, 'my nephew loves my things.'

'Good,' said Mr Holmes limply, and continued. 'Besides, even if I could afford to, I would not employ you. One of the species is bad enough. Two would frighten the horses.' He smiled his gentle infuriating smile. 'You and I, Mrs Lefarge . . .'

'Oh, do stop calling me Mrs Lefarge.'

Mr Holmes gave a dry little chuckle. 'You and I are not considered user-friendly, Mrs Lefarge. We should take lessons from the user-obsequious . . . The ad men, the PRs, the media personalities.' He rose to his feet. Small, studious and still smiling he showed her to the door, paused at the polished brass doorstep to give her more bad news.

'You realise, one can no longer buy Gauloises in this country?' He shook his neat head. 'However, fortunately my sister sends me a couple of packets a week secreted in . . .' Again that chuckle. 'But we mustn't tell all our secrets, must we, Mrs Lefarge? I like it here, love it, and fortunately so does my partner.'

'So you do have partner?' snapped Bianca.

'Ah yes, I do have a partner. He worships the sun.'

'There is too much hellish sun,' cried Bianca.

'If you say so.' Mr Holmes held out a small pink hand. 'Goodbye, Mrs Lefarge,' he said. 'Goodbye.'

Bianca could scarcely bear to touch the thing. She drove away twitching with disgust. Deranged. Mad as a coot. Two coots. And what about her plans, her behind-the-curtain visions; so clear, so bright, her hands realigning minuscule china fingers, adjusting rosebuds, making as good as new, though not, of course, as regards commercial value. But her clients, these grateful people who became her friends, who sought her help, would want their things restored, not sold.

'There's a wonderful woman in Meadowbank.' She could see friendships developing between the like-minded, goodwill and shared interests flowing on through the years.

She would borrow Gaby's Skoda again. Tomorrow, why not. I'll go further afield. I haven't scratched the surface. They can't all be mad.

Rosa, better late than never, was getting somewhere with the garden. In the past week she had hacked, slashed, cut back and divided. Like all foolish virgin gardeners, she had rushed to the garden centre for instant help; for colour, long flowering periods, showy perennials and a few architectural greys for the back. Her knees hurt but her garden glowed with strong-eyed marigolds, gentle verbenas and bright, splashy begonias. Her natives were trimmed, her edges cut.

She had gone outside originally because she could not bear to remain indoors. She wanted the wind in her hair and got it, she wanted peace of mind. In this she was not so successful, though work and a strong hoe had helped, as Kipling had told her it would, but not enough.

Rosa, to her surprise, was not happy. Shakespeare, as usual, had beaten her to it, '*Nought's had*,' she muttered crossly, '*all's spent, where our desire is got without content.*'

She had longed for Bianca to leave them and she had done so. All was going swimmingly at Webster Street, the new house was beautiful, its occupants pleased with life and the rent was paying off the mortgage, well almost.

She and Henry had got Bianca out of their hair with dignity, had extracted her gently, no knots, no painful tangles, not a tug. They had acted generously. They were free.

And more miserable than they had been since Andy's death.

There was something wrong with Henry. Unease hung like a pall over their comings and goings, their companionable silences became less so.

Rosa, digging with her red-handled grubber, came to a decision. She would speak to Henry tonight. Before she could help him he must tell her what was wrong. If he was clinically depressed he must seek help. Enough was enough and more than.

She looked up smiling as Bianca strode up the path, heaved herself up from her gardening frame and greeted her warmly. She gazed around her lovely show of colour. 'Looks nice, doesn't it?'

'Parks and Reserves.' Bianca sighed deeply. 'Annuals,' she murmured. 'Dear old annuals.'

There seemed little more to be said.

They sat side by side in silence on a garden bench left over from one of Rufus's less successful cut-price enterprises. Videos had been another. There was still a box of the things awaiting transport to the new house. It sat, appropriately labelled, in the garage beside Martin's ashes.

Midges danced in the late afternoon air, jigging, dissolving and jigging again. 'Crepuscular,' murmured Rosa who had lost heart with words and crosswords since Martin died. The cryptics in the paper, yes, but not his half-finished books. They waited beneath her handkerchiefs in her chest of drawers—the closest thing to a duchesse she could find. It occurred to her, watching the endless quivering of life, the disturbed air above the garden tap, that she could have told Martin about Henry's decline. Not his mother, not his son and certainly not the woman sitting rump by rump beside her. She could have told Martin. After a whisky, perhaps, when the final clue had been pencilled in.

Martin, Henry is behaving very oddly. She saw the friendly eyes, the concern. Then what? Nothing, nothing ever again. She shut her eyes.

'What?' said Bianca.

Rosa jumped slightly. 'What?'

'Oh for goodness' sake, you said something.'

'Oh. Crepuscular. It means twilight, or rather . . .'

'I realise that.'

More silence. Bianca wondered whether to tell her sister about Mr Holmes and decided against it. Rosa had never been any good at nuances.

Bianca put out a hand, plucked a lemon verbena leaf. An idea clicked into her brain, appeared from nowhere in the moment between the crushing of the leaf and its fragrance.

'What are you going to do with all the money Martin Brown left you?' she asked.

I have been expecting this. This is when I tell her I lied and I apologise. When I tell her I knew she would understand. When I agree my behaviour was inexcusable, one of those mad impulses, like a child really. That Martin hadn't a bean. That it was a joke. That I knew she would see the funny side.

'I haven't got it yet,' I mutter.

'Yes, but when you do?'

Now! I brace myself. 'I'm glad you mentioned it, Bianca. I've been meaning to tell you for some time . . .'

But Bianca had stopped listening. She was up and running with her idea; instant, vivid and good. Blow pots of spare fingers and glue and Mr Holmes and all his works. His balderdash, his pink hands, his gall, none of them mattered. All were irrelevant, completely irrelevant. There were better ways of making money. She put a hand on Rosa's thigh.

'The best thing, dear,' she said, 'would be for you to buy another villa and I'll do it up.'

'Bianca, I must tell you . . .' Rosa stopped, leapt to her feet to embrace Henry as he mooched slowly up the path. 'Hullo, darling,' she cried.

He detached himself gently. 'What must you tell Bianca?'

'We were talking about what Rosa is going to do with all

the money Martin Brown has left her.'

Henry changed his briefcase to the other hand, put it on the ground and looked at it. 'Ah,' he said.

Typical, absolutely typical of the wretched man to arrive at the wrong moment. There was no point in pursuing the splendid thought now. And perhaps it would be better to wait a little, to get her thoughts down on paper, to strengthen her arguments.

And at least she would get a gin. Two gins. Gaby and Rufus scarcely drank spirits and gin had gone through the roof since she had last bought any here. The bow-tied Jason at Liquorland had also asked her where she'd been for the last thirty years.

And that Bettina child would probably still be sitting around at Webster Street. She and Gaby spent hours smoking and drinking coffee at the kitchen table. There was nothing wrong with the child and Bianca could always go and sit with her things, but . . .

Henry picked up his briefcase. 'Gin,' he said.

Rosa turned on the sprinkler as she left. The midges regrouped, foamed higher as the drops fell.

Bianca had two strong gins and left.

Rosa lifted the remains of her glass to the collapsed figure in the chair. 'To Scrooge McDuck,' she said.

He gave a brief snort. 'Thank you. Any particular reason for the duck?'

'That's what you look like, lying there. If you could see yourself. You've shrunk, gone all hopeless-looking, halved in size.' Rosa took a sip of gin, remembered that she had meant to be gentle and kind to this man in need of help. It still came out wrong. 'What on earth's the matter with you, sitting there miserable as a bandicoot?'

'It was a duck a moment ago.'

'Tell me.'

Henry stirred, smiled at her concerned pink face. 'Why did you tell Bianca Martin had left you a lot of money?'

'It seemed a good idea at the time.'

'*The Heart Has Its Reasons*?'

This was too close for comfort, too perceptive, too like the lightning etc. Rosa sat straight. 'We're not talking about why I lied.'

Then whose lies were they talking about. Not his, surely. Henry was drained bone dry, exhausted. She couldn't mean that, not Rosa, his generous, loving Rosa. He gave a brief cough and waited.

'We're talking about why you've gone into some sort of decline. We're talking about how we should be happy and peaceful like we were, not talking much, not enough probably, but knowing it was all right, that we were on the same wavelength. That you didn't cheat or lie and nor did I, well not much. That you are, at heart, a decent man, generous even. You huff and puff but look what you did to help Bianca. That was a generous thing to do, very generous, though I've never been able to understand why you didn't discuss it with me first. You've been a good father, though again you won't talk, won't discuss Rufus. Let alone Gaby. I don't like Gaby. Do you like Gaby?'

He moved his hands. 'I . . .'

'There you are, you see! You don't know. And if you did know you probably wouldn't tell. Where have you *gone* Henry?'

He opened his mouth to tell her he didn't know and shut it. She was upset, deeply upset, her face pinker than ever, her eyes bright with tears. All his hopeless bewildered love flowed to her. He flopped onto the unicorn footstool beside her and took her hand. 'Rosa, my dear.'

She snatched it away.

'I must talk to you, Henry. I used to talk to Martin but he's dead.' She was crying now, noisily, her face blotched with damp and pain. 'And what was in his letter to you? You said you'd lost it.' She gave a deep, shuddering gasp and turned to stare. 'I don't believe that, Henry. I've never believed that for a moment.'

He walked to the window, stared at nothing. 'So what can I do?'

'Tell me what was in it.' She waited, listened to silence. 'It was Italy, wasn't it?'

He turned. 'Yes.'

She seemed smaller than ever in the large chair. A wide-eyed bush creature; small, gallant and fierce.

'A woman?'

'Yes.'

She had never felt like this before. Weak as a kitten, strong as a lion, appalled, humiliated and seething with rage, Rosa demanded facts—'Tell me,' she said.

'Twenty years!'

'Longer.'

The length of time is the thing. The most unforgivable thing of all. A life sentence of deceit.

When I was pregnant this deception began. When the woman remarried and not before it was ended. By her. Those are the facts. And all this, all this he has told me in *my own home.* It is better to die in your own bed but not much, less than much, if you're murdered.

I am going mad. Have gone.

And so I am and so I do and all these feelings rage and I am outraged. And then I begin to laugh, and I laugh and laugh and laugh and tears roll down and splash on my hands and my front and still I laugh.

Henry, not unnaturally, is alarmed. He gets water, wonders what to do, holds me in his arms, hushes and begs me for help and sanity. 'Rosa, darling Rosa, don't. Rosa, please.'

I calm down. I lie in his arms on the sofa where we have landed up. We are close, locked together like parents at airports awaiting bad news.

I sit up, blow my nose. 'After all,' I say, 'I had Martin.'

Henry is staring at me in disbelief which turns to horror. Rank terror. Terror I can see, hear, smell. 'You were lovers?'

'Yes. But not forever.'

'When?'

'When do you think? When you were away. He begged me for years but I wouldn't.' I think of my friend Martin, so much older, so much wiser. 'He knew, I suppose. About the woman?'

'Yes.'

This is it then. This is life. This is men. This is the love that needs a fall guy and I am it. I look at this stranger, this wet hen, this man. I shake my head.

'What a fool,' I say. 'What a stupid idiotic fool I've been.'

'No. Rosa. Rosa. I love you.'

'Thank you,' I say.

They talked for hours, they tossed about on a sea of words; words for recrimination, rage, betrayal. They struggled for air, half-drowning on the surface, they submerged and rose spluttering in despair.

They begged for reason, for sense, for understanding. They did not mention forgiveness. They clung to the wreckage.

'Do you want me to sleep somewhere else?' said Henry eventually.

'Oh, for God's sake,' snapped Rosa. 'And turn off the sprinkler.'

twelve

The gardening talents in Webster Street also combined well. Bianca knew about the cottage-garden effect desired, Gaby did not. Bianca was strong and Gaby stronger and Rufus took the stuff to the dump. Bianca's plan, easy care with colour and plenty of self-seeders, was approved. The last thing Gaby and Rufus wanted was to have to fart around in the section every weekend, especially as Gaby was looking for a job. Weekends were for unwinding, for lying on the as yet unlaid grass, for absorbing energy for the trip to the supermarket then on to the wine bar.

Gaby continued to be generous with the Skoda, was quite insistent that Bianca should have it once a week. Bianca owed herself a break, hell yes, and Gaby could shoot off any time.

Bianca accepted with thanks and was meticulous about petrol. She did not bother to tell Gaby or Rufus of her change of interest, that she had abandoned her search for a niche behind the velvet curtain of the antique world. She no longer sought Antiques, Collectibles or Colonials. She sought old villas in need of care and attention. She bought a map entitled *Auckland, City of Sails*, with the harbour bridge on the front, and set off every Monday on a treasure hunt which was hers alone. She bought her own *Herald* on real estate day and studied it with care, marked the possibles with her yellow highlighter, packed her lunch and set off with heart aglow. She was positive. Like Rufus she had no time for negative wimps. You could keep them.

She went to a different area each week, called first on any likely real estate vendors but ignored the obviously useless two-man outfits squeezed between TABs and Cambodian takeaways.

Having obtained the essentials of location and likely price of any villas for sale, she rejected offers of further assistance. But you won't have a key, they cried. Bianca explained that that would not be necessary at this stage. As she told Ken and Douglas and Trish and Soph, she just wanted to get a feel for the place. Make what her late husband used to call a 'recce'. Time spent on reconnaissance, he used to say, is never wasted. She would be back.

She kept careful notes in a small 3B1 notebook labelled *Bianca. Do not lose.*

Her sense of direction was a help. She had always done the navigating while Justin drove. He couldn't have managed in town without her, he told her every time they sailed over the hog's back on their way home. And she would smile and slip her hand under his on the wheel and be happy.

She learned quickly that she was too late for Freemans Bay or Ponsonby or even, she feared, Grey Lynn. She wasted no time on repining. She knew what she wanted: a villa at a reasonable price which Rosa could buy with the man's money and Bianca could do up. Her assistants in this enterprise were uncertain at the moment—Rufus and Gaby would both be working—but these details could be worked out later.

In the meantime she must get on to Henry about the title of Webster Street. This, again, would require thought. She would have to get Henry on his own and was concerned as to how to do this. She had scarcely seen him since the move. She had no illusions about future drives in the country or of his making unaccompanied visits to Webster Street, even if invited. Especially if invited. Rosa would have to come too. She would ask them for a meal when Gaby and Rufus were out, as they often were. She should have asked them before. Rosa had been very kind to her. She would get out the silver.

'But I don't want to!'

'It's her birthday.'

'I don't care if it's her annunciation. I'm not going.'

'You are. We both are.'

'Rosa.'

'Henry.'

They stared at each other in the misty bathroom mirror. Red-nosed, creased and disillusioned, two old faces stared back. Rosa picked up the nail scissors, cut a few misparted grey hairs from the left side and whirled them down the basin.

Her back was towards him as she bent over, pink and shiny and familiar as his own. More so.

'It's Martin's birthday too.'

'Oh.'

She turned to him, her face serious. She didn't want him to get it wrong.

'I'm just telling you. I'm not trying to . . . not bully you or anything. I'll go anyway. I can make up some lie.'

Tears rushed to his eyes. 'Oh, my dear heart.'

It was some time since they had clutched each other naked and upright.

One of the pleasures of competence is the pleasure of getting it done, of having plenty of time in hand, of never having to scramble or rush. Bianca had set the table in the morning with the Worcester which remained. The silver had been polished, the linen starched and she had done the flowers. The *blanquette* of veal had been made yesterday, whipped cream already glued the meringues, the coffee tray was laid. She had even found some proper dessert mints, elegant imported wafers of dark bitter chocolate with peppermint not given to ooze.

She sat upright in her wing-backed chair and gazed about the room. It was beautiful, this house, more beautiful than she could ever have hoped. She could have been in Titchfield, the wood was just as fine, her things as harmoniously placed as ever they had been. There were things to be done, certainly, the chintzes were worn, an ivory button handle had come off the bow-fronted commode, the longcase clock had yet to be set going. Some things were still packed owing to lack of space. But the feeling, the ambience, the mellowness was there. The glow of lives well lived and waited upon by others was evident in the deep sheen of the oak chest, the patina of the commode was there forever. Once things have that depth, that intensity of polish, only a quick buff up is required.

And Long Life is a godsend for silver.

Bianca realised she was having a Happy Birthday and would continue to do so when Rosa arrived. She was grateful to Rosa and, by extension, Henry, though she needn't go into that. Perhaps her birthday was not the night to bring up the question of the title. No.

The doorbell rang. It couldn't be them. Not at quarter past three.

Bianca, smiling and already into her blue, opened the door to excited strangers.

They introduced themselves. 'I'm Margie Dempster and this is Stephen.'

'How do you do.'

They wondered if they could just have another peep around. They realised that it was by appointment only, but they were over this way on account of Stephen's mother and they happened to have seen Mrs . . . in the garden, and they were so excited about the place, they just wondered . . .

Stephen agreed. Margie reiterated. If she wouldn't mind too much could they slip round for a second, seeing they were passing, and wasn't it looking *lovely*.

Bianca's hand clutched the warm polished brass of the door knob. Her breath had gone, gone completely.

'I don't know what you're talking about,' she gasped.

'But we've made an offer. Conditional on finance. We signed on Monday.'

'There's been some mistake,' panted Bianca. 'Go away. Go away at once,' she cried and slammed the door.

'Ask Bettina!' Margie screamed back. 'Ask Bettina and then see, you silly old . . .'

They banged, they knocked, they rang the bell, they shouted.

Bianca stumbled to her chair, hid her ears with her hands. Still, still she could hear them shouting. 'Go away,' she begged. 'Please, please go away. Oh dear God, please.'

She picked up the blue cardigan beside her and pressed it to her trembling lips. She was shaking with fright. Cold, cold as ice. She must put things on, keep warm. That is what you do when you've had a shock. You keep warm. You treat for shock and work things out. You don't panic. It was just a muddle. Some stupid muddle. It would be all right, quite all right. Yes. She sat motionless clutching the cardigan, her eyes focused on the tiny washing instructions label, the rest of the world a blur.

Warm Gentle
Machine wash
Do not wring
Do not tumble
Acrylic

How could it be acrylic? She never bought acrylic. Never. She couldn't stand acrylic. She bought wool. Pure wool. Always. Always, always. She banged the crumpled thing to her eyes with shaking hands and sobbed her heart out.

But not for long. She would stop this nonsense. She would ring Bettina. Bianca walked to the kitchen, poured herself a glass of the water and drank it slowly as she gazed out the window to the emergent back garden. She put out a hand to steady herself against the wall which had once screamed *Fuck off, Fraser* and no longer did.

'Clarion Real Estate, Bettina speaking,' sang the voice. 'Can I help you?'

'Bettina, this is Bianca Lefarge speaking.'

'Sure is. I recognised your voice. Lovely day.'

'Bettina, two people have just banged on the door wanting to see the house.'

'Oh, that's *bad*. I hate that when it's appointment only. Really, some people. We told everyone, we said. And anyway who's come now when we've got a conditional.'

'What!'

'Like I said, offer conditional on finance. Margie and Steve Dempster. Lovely couple. Signed on Monday.'

'Who signed?'

'Well, him and Roof.'

'I'm sorry to have to tell you, Bettina,' breathed Bianca, her knees weak with joy, her heart singing, 'but there's been some mistake. Rufus does not own the title.'

'How d'y'mean?'

'The title is owned by Rufus's father. Mr Henry Felton.'

Bettina's voice lifted. 'Mrs Lefarge, I've seen it. I don't want to be snippy, but what do you think I am? Some sort of nutcase who can't recognise a title? Believe me, there's no glitches in this one. Rufus owns it and Rufus signed it and if you don't mind, Mrs Lefarge, I'm a busy professional woman. Ask them. Ask Rufus.'

Panic seized her, panic and misery and heartbreak. She screamed down the telephone. 'You inveigled him, trapped him. I know my nephew. He's a good man, he loves me, he'd never, never . . . Oh, don't you tell me that, you . . . you. I've never liked you, hanging around, taking it all in, twisting Gaby and him round your little finger.'

Bettina gasped. 'Twisting Gaby? You must be joking. I'd as soon twist a python.' Her voice froze. 'As for *inveigling*. They didn't need any inveigling, Rufus nor Gaby, especially Gaby. I've never seen a sharper vendor. Keen as mustard. And frankly, Mrs Lefarge, I don't see why I should sit here being insulted by you, if you don't mind. Ask Rufus. Goodbye.'

Bianca put the receiver back in its cradle. Nothing, nothing in her whole life had been as bad as this. This was the worst. Andrew, the shoes, the horror, Justin's decline, all the insults and miseries of her life had been nothing compared with this. She was shaking all over as she tugged pale blue acrylic around her shoulders. She had nobody, nobody in the whole world. She knew that.

And nor do millions. Millions and millions and millions. Bianca squared her shoulders. She would get herself a gin. She would have a gin to help her think and she would work out what to do.

She walked slowly down the hall and reached for the bottle. It was virtually empty. Someone had drunk her gin. She saw them, Bettina, Phil, Gaby seated at the table, laughing, smoking, drinking her gin. Lifting glasses, clinking, congratulating themselves and each other. But not Rufus. Rufus had not been there. They had trapped him somehow. Inveigled. 'Rufus,' she moaned. 'Rufus.'

She poured the remaining gin into a kitchen glass, added a

slurp of water and drank it quickly. She would get some more. And cigarettes. She would work things out.

Webster Street, as Bettina had told them, was so handy. 'Slipper distance to the shops,' she had laughed.

The street was virtually empty, a sheet of newspaper sailed onto the road, was squashed by a woman cyclist in an orange parka who nodded. Bianca, her head throbbing, her heart torn, nodded back. The front door of a house opened, closed; cloud reflections drifted across the roof of its stick-on conservatory.

Jason, the young man with the bow-tie and the shaved head, greeted her with his usual enthusiasm.

'I want a large bottle of gin,' said Bianca. 'The largest you have.'

'Right on,' said Jason and moved to get it although it was self-service. Bianca knew this but she disliked carrying the naked bottle across yards of blue carpet to be decently camouflaged at the counter—or rather dumped into a yellow plastic bag shrieking Liquorland. There is something about old women and bottles of gin. Something with which Bianca did not wish to be associated. Toothless drunken old hags in old prints selling their wares, *Drunk for a penny, blind drunk for tuppence.*

She concentrated on the carpet. It was two-toned with squiggles like a cross-section of the human brain Justin had once shown her. She stayed staring until the bottle was safely encased then slid the money across without looking.

She cradled the bag in her arms, held it to her chest. All around were bottles, bottles for miles. Bottles to help the thought processes, to calm, to clarify.

'There you go,' smiled Jason.

'Yes. Yes, thank you.' She stood motionless, her heart screaming for help, her eyes on his shaven head. 'What is that style of haircut called, Jason?'

Jason gave an embarrassed yelp. 'Aw, a Number One.'

She looked at him thoughtfully, stared at his well-shaped head, his neat ears. Stood cuddling gin among nuts and nibbles and Twisties in racks.

'Why is it called that?'

'They use a number one blade, see. The razor.'

Bianca nodded. So fit, so nimble, so kind. 'I see.' She stood silent for a moment, then gazed into his eyes. 'It looks very handsome,' she said.

Jason's shy feet moved again. 'Thanks.' He clapped his hands together in bonhomie and dismissal, dipped his head at her purchase. 'Yeah, well. That'll give you plenty of needle.'

'Thank you,' murmured Bianca.

'Good as gold,' said Jason.

Henry and Rosa went for a swim on the way to Bianca's. Henry had suggested it. He would pick Rosa up after work and they could slip down to the beach, why not. There would be plenty of time. He made many suggestions for shared pleasures now, kept an eye out, spotted mild treats, small breaks in the dailiness of life: a cafe with good polenta, a newly opened wine bar overlooking the container wharf, a film. They were both aware that this had been Rosa's province. She had always been good at treats and seemed amused by his endeavours, had looked him in the eye over an unexpected glass of riesling last Thursday. 'Are we bonding, Henry? Is that what we're trying to do? Rebond?'

'I hope so.'

She smiled, shook her head. In tolerance or mild negation, but not, please God, in rejection.

The swims after work were good. What could be more therapeutic than to lie in the sun, to relax with his wife after a day at the warehouse pretending all was well between himself and Rufus, a day spent tiptoeing around a son who walked on eggshells. What better than to lie beside her, to sense her presence as she padded through sand to flop beside him, to put out a hand to her wet thigh. 'Good?'

'Mmmn.'

'Warmer than yesterday?'

'A bit.'

'Good, good.' They would get there, they would get there in the end.

He had not told her about the change of title and must do so immediately. He opened his eyes to see her drying her wet head on an ancient beach towel of Carmen Miranda plus fruit. Rosa dropped it, put both hands to her mouth and yawned, her eyes on the frill of white surf edging blue and Rangitoto beyond.

'I wonder why the Maoris called it Bloody Head,' she said dreamily. 'We should climb it one day.'

There you are, you see. Straws in the wind, good omens waving. It would all be all right. He spoke quickly while it still was. 'I have changed the title to Webster Street. Made it over to Rufus.'

'Why on earth?'

An obvious question, and one not easy to answer. I did it to save you pain. I did it because our son exercised moral blackmail. I did it because I am who I am. The fact that you now know my secret anyway is because my pitch has been queered by your ex lover, the good, the loyal, Martin Fucking Brown, God rot his soul but don't bother. Martin Brown, of all people. An old man with half a gut, reeking of nicotine and a bore to boot. The very thought made him ill.

'Why didn't you *tell* me?' she cried into the silence.

Another difficult question, and equally impossible to answer. He dragged his mind back from betrayal. His voice was gentle as he sidestepped. 'Have you any objections?'

Rosa tossed her head. Drops of seawater fell on her freckled chest, her rounded arms as she swung towards him.

'Yes!' she cried. 'Yes, I do.'

'Such as?'

She gave a shuddering gasp. 'Don't you understand? No, you've never understood. You won't see. All his life I have worried about Rufus. I have worried whether perhaps he was . . .'

Was what? Feckless? Self-centred? Aren't they all. The young are meant to be. But was Rufus perhaps too sharp, too quick, too obsessed with instant wealth?

She could not say it. Loyalty as well as love forbade it. This was her secret. She was the only one who knew. And what did she mean, knew? There was nothing to know, nothing. Just that she loved Rufus and always had and always would. To tell, even to mention her fears was not only disloyal to him; suspicions, however vague, proliferate once shared, spread like bushfires and destroy. She had not even told Martin.

'It's Bianca,' she said finally. 'What if he, they, sell the house? You've made Bianca vulnerable, exposed to Gaby, of all people.'

'No. I made him put it in writing. He will not sell the house without consulting Bianca.'

Rosa shivered. 'Why did you do that?' she whispered.

'Because I'm not sure I trust him,' said Henry.

Her mouth dropped. At the statement, yes, but more, much more because Henry had made it. Henry, who had never been prepared to discuss his son, who knew Rufus would be all right, Henry *knew*. 'Oh, Henry,' she cried and flung herself at him.

'I didn't want to worry you,' he said over her shoulder to a gawking youth with a frisbee. Wet, salty, uncomfortable and uncomforted, she lay still.

'You'll have to tell her tonight,' she muttered.

'Yes.'

'How can you! How can you possibly?'

'I will.'

'It's her birthday.'

'You said.'

They picked up their sandy towels and trailed back to the changing sheds and cold showers and the rush hour.

Bianca sat upright in the wing-backed chair drinking gin. She had never put her feet up as Rosa did, had never flopped about and had no intention of starting now. She had made notes in her 3B1 notebook to clear her mind. There was much to think about. She would tell Rosa and Henry tonight of the perfidy of their son, what he had done, how he had done it. Though obviously it was Gaby. Bianca had never liked her, never. She had known, from the first moment she had seen her in those ghastly boots she had known, Gaby was sly, manipulative and not to be trusted. You had only to look at her. Those eyes too close together, too muddy. The eyes, she told her precariously balanced gin, are the windows of the soul.

She lit another cigarette, drank deeply. Oh, but gin was good. She looked at it, oily, beautiful and subtle to the tongue. The juniper berries, presumably, there was a picture on the label. But how do you know if you haven't tasted junipers? What did the tree look like, the bearer of these blue-black treasures? '*Oh ruddier than the cherry*,' she sang, '*Oh sweeter than the berry*.' There were no more words no more at all. She started again. '*Oh ruddier than the cherry*,' she sang and burst into tears.

This would not do.

She lifted her glass, lit another cigarette, opened her notebook once more and wrote slowly and carefully.

1. Tell Henry re Rufus.

2. Rosa to buy old villa.

3. Bianca to . . .

She sat up quickly, wiped ash from her blue front. How disgusting, she was a tidy smoker. Gaby had told her, she had said . . . what had she said? Something. It didn't matter. Nothing that terrible person said mattered. Person, not woman. Not woman, like Justin's woman. Justin against the light. '*Moon of* gladness *by night, strength and joy thou art to me*,' she sang, beating time with her cigarette like Miss Blennerhasset in senior choir. Though not really. Miss Blennerhasset hadn't had a cigarette. Bianca giggled, became serious. Miss Blennerhasset had had bad breath. Bianca couldn't be doing with bad breath. You could keep it. She giggled again, sobbed. There had been no gladness by night, no strength and joy at the end. Nothing.

Her notebook slipped to one side to lie beside the blue cardigan.

She noted with surprise that her glass was empty, stood up with stately care and walked down the wide hall to the kitchen, her hand checking the wall as she went. She poured the gin from the depleted open bottle, watched with approval as the water mingled. Oil and water don't mix but they do when necessary, they do when required to assist thought, to make plans. There was something, some reason, something to do with Henry . . . She would wait till she got back to her chair.

It had gone, the reason why Rosa would now have to buy the villa. Why she would be *duty-bound*. Bound by duty. Trussed. Men used to wear trusses. There had been advertisements in the *Auckland Weekly News*, strange little pictures at the side depicting appliances which could be sent for and which would arrive under plain cover. She would ask Henry, stupid old Henry. Henry, she would say, do men truss these days? Now that was funny, that was very funny. To truss or not to truss. To fuss or not to fuss. Trussy fussy.

She was dreamy now, dreamy and happy and strangely tired. She gazed around the room at the warm light flowing past calico curtains made by Rosa. Bianca had been disgusted at first (calico!) but they were cheap and there had been no fee for the making. Rosa had been only too happy to have been of some use. The curtains looked well, formed a muted backdrop for her things. Her things were here.

'Yes,' she whispered. 'Yes.'

'Fire engine,' said Rosa.

Henry, who had already pulled to the side of the road, nodded.

The engine shot past them, wailing its anguish into the distance as it spun around a corner in the direction of Webster Street.

'Bianca!' screamed Rosa.

He was ahead of her, speeding, cutting corners, hurtling after the thundering thing till it turned in to an adjacent street. Oh God, thank you, God.

Henry slowed for a second, but no more. 'Christ!'

The Webster Street house was well away, flames shooting skywards. They fell out of the car.

'Towels,' he yelled through the roar, 'get the wet towels. The hose.'

The Sex Pistols fan next door had already done so. Buckets were being filled, chain gangs begun. 'On the *door*,' yelled Henry, 'on the door.' He grabbed one of the wet towels, wrapped it around his fist and slammed it through the glass panel at the side of the door. Smoke billowed out as he unsnibbed the lock, the brass knob was red hot. He stumbled, stepped back and tried again. The door swung open, smoke and powdered plaster surged around them.

'Go away,' he screamed at Rosa's terrified face.

'Back,' yelled someone. 'Everyone back.'

The fan stood firm, continued playing the hose on Henry and the front door. Someone grabbed Rosa. 'Come back, you can't help.' Rosa punched the woman in the chest and dropped to her knees to follow Henry.

The fire engine arrived; efficient, well-trained men connected the hydrant and took control.

'Anyone inside?' they yelled at the youth.

'Yeah, two or three. Two old guys have just gone in.'

'In this lot? Jeeze!'

Bianca lay face down in the hall. The sitting room ceiling caved in as Henry and Rosa began dragging her out, showering them with plaster and burning debris. The three of them lay motionless beneath black smoke, drenched by water blasting from the firemen's hoses, surrounded by the roar of fire from the gutted sitting room and the creaks and tearing rumbles of the hall collapsing about them. The firemen saved them, picked them up bodily in their protected arms and carried them to safety like errant children beguiled by matches. They should not have gone in.

Bianca was dead.

Each cubicle in intensive care was equipped with its own ventilator, intravenous lines and ECG monitor. The lifesaving technology terrified him. Rufus knew about technology but not this stuff. These winking, blinking, green-eyed monitors appalled him, these ventilators, drips and draining bottles, these tubes in grey faces.

He came every day. He moved forward, breathless with fright, past people fighting for their lives. You don't get to intensive care unless you're fighting for your life.

Henry and Rosa lay in adjacent beds. Smoke inhalation had caused adult respiratory distress syndrome. They both had extensive superficial burns plus a certain amount of deep dermal burns, hands mostly. Less serious in Rosa's case. With luck, the registrar had told him, they would recover. Rosa certainly. They would be kept ventilated and endotracheal tubes were essential at this stage as well as drips. 'So they can't speak, of course.'

'No,' said Rufus. 'No.'

He had stood speechless between the two beds for days, had watched the mouths around tubes, the blistered crackling skin.

'Burns are always a bit of a shock,' smiled the registrar, 'but they're both heavily sedated.'

'Good. Good.'

The young nurse greeted him smiling. 'They've both been extubated,' she said. 'They might even talk.' She touched his arm. 'Ten minutes. Okay?'

He nodded. They didn't look any better, no better at all. As always, he didn't know which bed to stand beside, which parent to attend. Their eyes were shut. Henry's mouth a black hole.

Rufus's eyes filled with tears. 'Dad?' he said eventually. 'Mum?'

He sat on the edge of the chair beside Rosa, weeping at the sight of the olds. The half-dead olds. At Henry's swollen and hairless head. At Rosa. Sweet Jesus, how had it all happened, how had it come to this?

'Mum?' he said again. 'Dad?'

They opened their eyes together as though he had pushed a button. Henry had no eyebrows; Rosa no lashes.

Rosa's cracked lips moved. He leaned forward.

'Gaby?' she whispered. 'Where's Gaby?'

'I don't know.'

Her eyes closed. The hand lying on the cover was bandaged. Hidden from sight. Not human at all.

He gave a compulsive sob. 'I'm sorry.'

Rosa's tongue licked. 'Bianca's dead.'

'I know, I know. Oh, my God, Mum. I didn't . . . You've got to believe me, Mum.'

Her head moved.

'*Mum.*'

Her bald eyes stared at him. 'Not now, Rufus. No. Not now.'

Henry held out an enormous bandaged hand. 'No, Rosa.' He gasped, tried again. 'It wasn't his fault. None of it. No.'

His eyes closed.